K

Leabharlann Chathair Phort Láirge

Telephone: 051-309975 941·0850922

ROYAL SUBJECTS

A Biographer's Encounters

THEO ARONSON

Cartoons by Gary

SIDGWICK & JACKSON

First published 2000 by Sidgwick & Jackson
an imprint of Macmillan Publishers Ltd
25 Eccleston Place, London SW1W 9NF
Basingstoke and Oxford
Associated companies throughout the world
www.macmillan.co.uk

ISBN 0 283 07276 8

Copyright © Theo Aronson 2000

The right of Theo Aronson to be identified as the
author of this work has been asserted by him in accordance
with the Copyright, Designs and Patents Act 1988.

Cartoon copyright © Gary 2000

3 5 7 9 8 6 4 2

A CIP catalogue record for this book is available from
the British Library.

Typeset by SetSystems Ltd, Saffron Walden, Essex
Printed and bound in Great Britain by
Mackays of Chatham plc, Chatham, Kent

For Brian

CONTENTS

Author's Note

A FAMOUS EIGHTEENTH-CENTURY satirist, celebrated for portraying the reigning monarch, George III, as a garrulous simpleton, was once accused of being 'a very bad subject' to the King. He didn't know about that, answered the satirist, 'but I *do* know that the King has been a devilish good subject for me'.

For over thirty-five years various kings, and their families, have proved to be devilish good subjects for me. Ever since the publication of my first book, *The Golden Bees: The Story of the Bonapartes*, I have written about the reigning, or sometimes deposed and exiled, royal houses of Europe. I have dealt with the Bonapartes, the Spanish Bourbons, the German Kaisers, the Coburgs of Belgium and the Stuart Pretenders, as well as with Queen Victoria and her various descendants.

In the main, these books have been historical biographies, concerned with people in the past but, in the course of the last two decades, I have written about various contemporary members of the British royal family. These biographies are: *Princess Alice, Countess of Athlone; The Royal Family: Years of Transition; The Royal Family at War* and *Princess Margaret*.

While researching and writing these books, I have been given almost unprecedented access to royal circles. I have interviewed major and minor members of the royal family, members of the royal households, as well as various officials, servants, friends and others whose lives are in some way connected with the monarchy. There are several reasons for this unusual access. One was my friendship with Princess Alice, Countess of Athlone. Another was that, having been born in South Africa, I was something of an outsider, unrestricted by the British class system. In my cheerfully uninhibited way, I simply asked for interviews. I was also helped, I imagine, by the fact that I was already an established historical biographer.

During this twenty-year period I have kept notes of all my interviews, experiences and correspondence; not only concerning these four more contemporary studies but all the royal books I have written during this time. What follows is not so much a diary as a series of wide-ranging notes, scribbled down at the time and written up and often expanded at a later date. I have also included the occasional flashback to my previous encounters with royalty.

These two decades coincide with an especially turbulent period in the history of the British royal family. In 1977, just before I embarked on these various royal encounters, Queen Elizabeth II celebrated her Silver Jubilee: arguably the high point of her reign. After that, things started to go downhill. By the time these notebooks end, the monarchy had embarked on a determined and sometimes desperate attempt to make itself more relevant to contemporary life. Inevitably, something of this evolutionary process is reflected in these notes.

The focus throughout these notes is on the researching, writing and promoting of these books; only where my personal life affects, or is affected by, my work is it touched upon. But I have spared the reader the longueurs of a writer's life: the days at the desk, the desperation, the frustrations, the boredom of proof-reading and indexing, the battles with the word processor. Rather, I have concentrated on whatever I have found amusing, entertaining, interesting and sometimes poignant. It is a light-hearted look at two worlds seldom glimpsed by most people: the world of a writer of the royal biography and of the still arcane world inhabited by members of the royal family.

All in all, I have set out to present a unique, lively and often irreverent record: a quite different slant on the royals and on writing about them.

PART I

'She had such get-up-and-go'

The Queen Mother on Princess Alice, Countess of Athlone

London, 19 September 1979

LUNCH WITH GERALD [Gerald Pollinger, my then literary agent] at Verry's in Regent Street. One thing about Gerald; you always get a decent lunch. We are meeting to decide on a subject for my next book. Am subjected to the usual author's humiliation of having every suggestion, no matter how enticingly put, turned down. Am even more worried about this ritual than usual. Although I've been a full-time non-fiction writer for over fifteen years and have made a pretty good living, I can still never see any reason why a publisher should want another book from me. And last month's move — from South Africa back to Britain — has been expensive and unsettling. On top of all this, Cassell [publishers of my last eight books] seems to be on the verge of collapse. My last idea — for a book on various American women who married into European royalty — which was enthusiastically welcomed by Cassell's previous editor-in-chief, has just been turned down by his successor. They need something 'more commercially viable'. Don't we all? Besides, I hate not having anything to do. If I don't write I drive everyone, especially Brian [fellow writer Brian Roberts], mad.

Over coffee, with time running out and still no decision, I put forward, very tentatively by now, the suggestion for a book on the 96-year-old Princess Alice, Countess of Athlone, Queen Victoria's last surviving granddaughter. I have known her for the last six years and have kept notes of all our conversations. Gerald immediately comes to life. 'Now that's more like it,' he says. 'I can get you a serialization with that.' Double brandies are ordered, the atmosphere lifts and we get down to details. He brushes aside my hesitations about the book being a betrayal of friendship. 'Somebody's going to do it,' he insists. 'I'm sure that she had rather you did it.' He instructs me to write to the Princess as soon as possible to 'stake my claim'. I should explain to HRH that I would be prepared to write either an official life, with full access to private papers, or a less formal book, with her sanction and help. The latter, in fact, is what I would prefer. I quail at the prospect of any prolonged contact with that uptight Sir Robin Mackworth-Young, the Queen's Librarian.

I weave out into Regent Street in a much more cheerful frame of mind.

20 September 1979

I get a suitably respectful letter off to Princess Alice at Kensington Palace. The trick is to use enough 'Your Royal Highnesses' without sounding smarmy. The body of it reads like this:

'I wonder if I could ask a favour of Your Royal Highness? My publishers are very anxious for me to write the story of your life [this isn't strictly true: Cassell know nothing about it but I thought that the Princess might be put off by the word 'agent'; it sounds somewhat shifty] and I have told them that, as I would not consider doing so without your permission, I would write to ask for Your Royal Highness's views on this matter. I have also told them that I would undertake it only if you were allowed full approval of the finished manuscript.

'I apologize if this request is in any way an intrusion, and will fully understand if Your Royal Highness would rather that I did not write the book. But may I say how very much I would like to do it, and I am sure that it will make a most fascinating study.'

Well, we shall see.

Mevagissy, Cornwall, 8 October 1979

Brian and I are living in one of Ronald Strauss's cottages. He's letting us stay here until we find a place of our own. We are tempted to buy one of the houses by the harbour but I suppose it would be a mistake to live so far from London. In any case, those screeching seagulls would drive us mad.

Still no reply from Princess Alice. It's been almost three weeks since I wrote. On our walk along the cliffs today we talk about our first meeting with HRH. It was six years ago, in January 1974, when she was on her annual visit to South Africa. We were then living in Kommetjie, a fishing village on the Atlantic coast, thirty miles from Cape Town. The Princess was spending a couple of weeks with Kathleen Murray on her apple farm at Elgin, about seventy miles from us. In common with most minor – and some major – royals, Princess Alice was not above making use of her elevated status to cultivate rich friends. She had just read my book *Grandmama of Europe: The Crowned Descendants of Queen Victoria* and wanted to meet me. So Kathleen Murray invited us to tea one afternoon. It was blazing hot; so hot that the thought of driving all the way to Elgin in long trousers was unthinkable. So we set out in shorts, parked under some trees near the farm gates and wriggled into shirts, ties, long trousers and jackets. As we crossed the stoep (verandah) of Kathleen Murray's neo-Cape Dutch house, I caught a glimpse of Princess Alice watching our arrival through a window.

Kathleen Murray, a heavily built woman ('only eighty-three', the then ninety-year-old Princess Alice was later to say to me, 'and just letting herself *go*') was, as always, very welcoming. Joan Lascelles, who was HRH's lady-in-waiting and companion, charged into the room to announce that the Princess wouldn't be long. I afterwards discovered that this was all part of a charade to build up the Princess's entrance: Joan Lascelles did this every time. I have sometimes spotted HRH, quite ready, lurking behind a door. I assumed Joan Lascelles to be in her sixties but she must have been over eighty – tall, angular, very talkative and assured. She looked what she was: a tough, upper-class spinster.

The first impression of Princess Alice was of smallness and fragility. She was very bent, very brittle-looking, with stick-like legs. The second impression was of bandbox elegance. She was wearing a pale silk dress. Her silver hair was drawn simply back from her face. Her profile was aquiline, her whole air very patrician, very royal. Strangely enough, she was probably better-looking in old age than in her youth, when she had a rather doll-like prettiness.

But she was anything but a frail and unapproachable old lady. On the contrary, she was vivacious, friendly, full of talk. I had to keep reminding myself that this was Queen Victoria's and – still more incredible – Prince Albert's granddaughter. Prince Albert had been dead for well over a century by the time I met this granddaughter of his.

We spoke, inevitably, about Queen Victoria. This is her great party piece. I signed the Princess's copy of my *Grand-mama of Europe*. On the jacket of the book is a reproduction of the Tuxen painting of Queen Victoria's vast family at the time of the Queen's Golden Jubilee in 1887. 'That's me,' announced Princess Alice, pointing to the little figure in a white dress handing a posy to the old Queen. 'I'm the only one who's still alive.' She was full of information, often highly uncomplimentary, about her various royal contemporaries.

The Princess is very deaf. Her way of coping with this is to take over the conversation. She holds the floor; you never get a word in with HRH. So while we bellowed the occasional remark, she babbled happily on.

During tea (trolley, silver teapot, cake stands, et al.) the Princess was telling us how much South African roads had improved since the 1920s when her late husband, the Earl of Athlone (Queen Mary's brother), had been Governor-General. 'They used to go up, and they used to go down,' she explained with a characteristic sweep of her hand which sent a cup of tea flying. Without even looking at the mess, HRH continued talking. Kathleen Murray rang for the maid. While the maid, who had a huge bum, was mopping up the spilt tea, she turned rather sharply and knocked over a vase of arum lilies. But even with the floor awash with water, the Princess kept her composure. She simply lifted her feet off the floor a fraction and went on with her story.

A few days later, when we were back in Kommetjie, Ann Seeliger told us that she had met 'two old ladies' on the beach who had wanted to know 'where Mr Aronson lived'. From Ann's description they were clearly Princess Alice and Joan Lascelles. HRH had, by then, moved to the De Beers' house [a holiday home belonging to the mining company] in nearby Muizenberg.

This sort of curiosity was very typical of Princess Alice. Equally typical was the frankness with which she admitted it. 'I've been spying on you,' she announced when we next met.

27 October 1979

This morning, just as I have decided that HRH is going to ignore my request, an answer arrives from Kensington Palace. It is written by Joan Lascelles. She is full of apologies for the delay: the Princess's secretary has been away. Princess Alice, now ninety-six, is 'not terribly well' but Sir Henry [Colonel Sir Henry Abel Smith, HRH's son-in-law] is 'most interested' in the idea. Joan Lascelles suggests that I contact Sir Henry when I'm next in London to arrange a meeting to discuss things.

As I loathe meetings and discussions – I am bad at them and they are invariably a waste of valuable time – I decide instead to send Sir Henry an informal synopsis of the projected book.

Monkton Deverill, Wiltshire, 1 November 1979

We are staying here with Alan Hartford and have bought a funny old house in nearby Frome (pronounced, for some reason, Froom), a market town in Somerset, about fifteen miles south of Bath. The house, built in the early 1700s, was buggered up in the late 1960s. In the living room the sash windows have been replaced by some especially nasty modern ones. But at least they let in more light and, as we didn't do the replacing, our consciences are clear. The house is called North Knoll Cottage. It is three-storeyed and stands in the middle of the town, bang on the old road to Bath. We are told that it was once a coaching inn at which the horses were changed: in fact, the floor of the large downstairs storeroom is still cobbled. Have also been told that from this storeroom a secret tunnel leads all the way to the village of Beckington, three miles away. I don't believe a word of it. Why the hell should there be a tunnel to Beckington?

The advantages of the house are that it has a sizeable entrance hall, a very large living room, two loos, a couple of rooms which will do as studies, two more bedrooms and a private, walled garden which I plan to have paved. No more lawn-mowing for me.

Strangely enough, when we were visiting Britain from South Africa last year and again staying with Alan, we had parked our hired car in Frome. It had refused to start and we had to call the AA to get us going again. The spot where we had parked was almost opposite the house we have now bought. So we must have seen it. [I must have told someone this story because it later appeared in a book called something like *Strange Coincidences*.]

Am glad that the house-hunting is over. Brian has just heard that Hamish Hamilton are delighted with his latest proposal — for a book to be called *The Mad Bad Line: The family of Lord Alfred Douglas* — which means he must start work soon. (In the old days, before we were both published writers, we used to celebrate even a kindly worded rejection with a meal out; nowadays a firm commission merits, at best, a bottle of wine.) I am hoping that, all going well, the first of my books to be written in North Knoll Cottage will be *Princess Alice: Countess of Athlone*.

Frome, 24 February 1980

As I have still had no reply from Sir Henry Abel Smith (and I suspect that the Princess herself is now too frail to take an active interest) I have decided to write the book anyway, with or without HRH's sanction or her family's co-operation. After all, I probably know her as well, even better, than any other biographer and have made copious notes of our conversations. Am also very much at home with her family background and with her years as the Governor-General's wife in South Africa. Have already started research and, as — for a royal — the Princess has led a far from conventional life, I am sure that the book will make interesting reading.

So I will write a full synopsis and get it off to Anne Carter [my editor at Cassell] tomorrow.

28 February 1980

This morning brings an enthusiastic letter from Anne Carter.
She says that my synopsis provides an odd coincidence. 'Just
over a year ago, we wrote to Princess Alice asking whether
she would allow us to commissiom a suitable author to write
her official biography. To which letter we got a polite "no"
and no indication as to whether or not one was being
considered. So you see you are preaching to the converted
when you say that a biography of her would make a
fascinating book, as indeed your synopsis bears out.'

Having dealt with various details, Anne expresses the hope
that I am not 'talking about publication on the centenary of
the Princess's birth in the belief that she will survive till then,
but surely the book should be written as soon as possible
since at ninety-seven she must be pretty frail and, not to be
ghoulish, the sooner it is published the better.'

17 March 1980

Having written to Anne Carter to explain the situation and
my progress to date, I get another letter off to Sir Henry to
ask if he has had time to consider my proposal for a life of
the Princess. As a little bribery always helps in these situations, I send him a gift copy of my *Grandmama of Europe*.

20 March 1980

A reply from Sir Henry's lawyers to say that he is 'abroad' and that they will give him my letter as soon as he returns. A damn nuisance. [Have since learned that he was away for several months on his farm in Ian Smith's Rhodesia; a fact that he is understandably anxious to keep quiet.]

3 April 1980

Today's letter from Sir Henry is kind but not really encouraging. 'The question of a biography of Princess Alice and the timing of it must be decided by the Powers that be,' he writes. 'I will certainly mention your name, when the question is discussed.' [Have since come to appreciate that all these fringe members of the royal family are terrified of doing anything that might upset the Queen.]

I write to Anne Carter to fill her in on these developments and to suggest that I go ahead and write the book anyway. I also tell her that in order to keep everything above board, I will be writing to Sir Henry to tell him exactly what I am doing. This is what I say to him:

'With regard to the biography of Princess Alice, I understand your position perfectly and I would not like to bother you any further with this. However, as my publishers are urging me to start the book, I thought that it would be only fair to let you know that I am going ahead. I will not claim this to be, in any way, an official biography but, as I said in my letter, I plan to make it a sympathetic and responsible study.

'If Her Royal Highness would like to see the completed manuscript before it is published, I would be only too willing to show it to her.'

Also write to Joan Lascelles to fill her in. I feel that I should keep in touch with her as she has been so sympathetic.

Can't say that I am really happy with things as they now stand, but what else can I do?

18 April 1980

Spend the morning working in the little walled side garden. Four hours of hard physical labour brings – as it usually does – not only its own reward but another, more tangible, one. With the midday post comes a letter from Sir Henry. Having, I presume, been in touch with the 'Powers that be' (Who? The Royal Archives? The Queen?), Sir Henry is ready to give the book his sanction. Although Princess Alice does not want 'anything in the way of an official biography' he would be quite happy to arrange for me to receive 'the same assistance as would be afforded to any serious writer engaged on such a project'. The Royal Archives at Windsor would be glad to do what they could and he would be ready to help me as much as he was able.

Will write to Anne Carter to give her the good news.

26 April 1980

'Hooray for your letter of 21 April,' writes Anne. 'That really is the best possible news. You seem to have finished up with all the advantages of an official biography and none of the disadvantages ... Congratulations on doing so well.'

The whole business has taken over seven months. It's just as well that I've been busy working on the book all this time.

4 May 1980

Have been reading my notes about Princess Alice's first visit to us at Kommetjie. It was memorable for all the wrong reasons. She and Joan Lascelles came to tea. At that time we had a tenant in our garden cottage. Pale and plump, he tended to put in an appearance at all the wrong moments. This was certainly true of the day of HRH's visit. At the very moment that, walking stick first, she battled out of the car (lent to her by De Beers), the tenant, unshaven and in vest and bathing trunks, decided to come out and lean over his gate. Definitely a lowering of whatever tone we were managing to muster. The Princess, with that inborn noblesse oblige, immediately crossed over to speak to him. 'Does he belong to you?' she asked us afterwards. 'Very sensibly dressed for the weather.' We, of course, were sweating in collars, ties and jackets.

We had invited Norah Henshilwood, the doyenne of Kommetjie, to meet the Princess. Norah was thrilled about this. She had last seen the Princess, forty-five years before, at the Athlones' farewell ball in the Cape Town city hall. As HRH was about to enter our sitting room, she stumbled over the doorstep and would have gone sprawling if Norah hadn't, at that moment, been shaking her hand and sinking into a deep curtsey. What if the Princess had fallen and broken a hip? What a drama! What *publicity!*

Throughout tea, the Princess's hearing aid kept playing up. This meant that conversation, never easy because of HRH's deafness, was constantly being interrupted by ear-piercing whines. 'She should have got a National Health one,' announced Joan Lascelles. 'We're told they're *frightfully* good.'

Both the Princess and Joan Lascelles were fascinated by the fact that the fading film star, Linda Christian, was visiting South Africa. The actress was being escorted by a local politician named John Wiley. Was she destined, wondered HRH, to become his fifth wife? [Some years later John Wiley, who was an outspoken racist with equally outspoken views on footballers hugging each other, committed suicide on being accused of sodomizing an Indian boy.]

Princess Alice's views on the South African political situation were exactly what one would expect of a British princess in her nineties. She simply could not understand the worldwide disapproval of apartheid. She felt that the South African government was generally misunderstood and misrepresented. She found the Afrikaners, whom she always called the 'Boers', charming (indeed, the Nationalist government courted her — as Queen Elizabeth II's great-aunt — assiduously) and the Blacks or 'Natives' — by which she meant the maids and chauffeurs in the various wealthy homes in which she stayed — all blissfully happy and contented.

One of her heroes is the late Field Marshal Smuts. Part world statesman, part visionary, part simple son of the veld and a fawning venerator of royalty, Smuts was greatly admired by the members of the British royal family. The Princess had recently been an honoured guest at the unveiling of a new statue of Smuts in Cape Town – a blandly representational work commissioned by various city worthies who had been horrified by an earlier, more expressionistic memorial to their hero. To her credit the Princess, who knows something about art, hated this new conventional statue. 'It makes him look so small and tight,' she said.

She had a good story to tell about Issie Smuts, the Field Marshal's wife. Unlike her celebrated husband, Mrs Smuts was a dowdy little woman of simple tastes who was quite ready to stay at home, well out of the limelight. In the 1920s, when Lord Athlone had been Governor-General, the vice-regal couple, with their interest in wild flowers and wild animals, had loved going on safari. They never minded how hot or dusty or uncomfortable it was and would happily sleep in their car or at the side of the road. The only thing that the always fastidious Princess Alice had found difficult during these journeys was getting her underwear laundered. One day she was telling Mrs Smuts about this difficulty. 'You must do what I do, my dear,' advised Mrs Smuts. 'Always wear black underwear. It never shows the dirt.'

27 August 1980

These months of research have been greatly enlivened by an avalanche of letters in reply to my requests – in newspapers in Canada, South Africa and Jamaica – for memories of Princess Alice. The writers range from middle-aged women who, as girls, once presented a bouquet to the Princess (invariably she looked like 'a fairy princess' or 'a piece of Dresden china', and if I get one more letter saying that the child was disappointed because the Princess wasn't wearing a crown, I shall scream) through colonial governors, aides-de-camp and professors to long-standing friends.

Some of the letters are hilarious. Many women give detailed descriptions of what they themselves wore at vice-regal balls or garden parties, with hardly a word about Their Excellencies. Some even send recent photographs of themselves in the hope, I imagine, that they will appear in the book. One touching note from an African woman in Johannesburg whose mother once worked in the kitchen of Government House in Pretoria during the Athlones' term, enclosing her mother's reference. Her letter is addressed to 'Lady Theo Aronson'.

There is an extraordinary letter from a woman in Canada who claims to be the great-granddaughter of Queen Victoria by a Lord Young. Apparently the sexually hyperactive Lord Young fathered not only the writer's grandmother and the future Edward VII, but Edward VII's queen, Alexandra, as well. This would have made King Edward VII and Queen Alexandra brother and sister. If this truth were ever to be revealed, the writer assures me, there would be 'a revolution in England'. (I have lost count of the times correspondents have warned me that there would be a revolution in this or that country if the truth about their own royal parentage were ever to become known.) The fact that this particular scandal 'did not appear in history books' was entirely due to the machinations of Queen Mary. It was she who prevented her eldest son (by now the writer has got her Edwards mixed) from revealing his true parentage. She ends by wishing me 'lots of luck' with my book on 'HRH Princess Alice, half-sister to my grandmother Christine Young, daughter of HRH Queen Victoria and Lord Young'.

London, 6 October 1980

To Kensington Palace to see Princess Alice's secretary, Mary Goldie. This is our first meeting as Miss Goldie has never been present during my various visits to HRH. As one enters the palace courtyard through the archway under the clock tower, the front door of the Princess's apartment is on the left. This has been Princess Alice's only home since the Athlones came back after his spell as Governor-General of Canada during the Second World War. He died in 1957. The apartment – called Clock House – is on four floors; its atmosphere is dignified but – like the Princess – light-hearted.

The prelude to my meeting with Miss Goldie is hilarious. The butler leads me upstairs and, on the landing, I am greeted by a middle-aged woman whom I assume to be Miss Goldie. She mumbles something; I mumble something; she tells me that I am expected and asks me to follow her. Just as I am about to enter what I afterwards realize to be Princess Alice's bedroom, there is a shout from a nearby doorway. The real Miss Goldie flies out and whisks me away. It appears that HRH is running a temperature and that the woman I assumed to be Mary Goldie is a nurse who, in turn, assumed that I was the doctor. (This is not the first time I have been mistaken for a doctor; a woman once said it was because I had 'clean clothes and a bedside manner'.) Miss Goldie leads me firmly downstairs into the late Lord Athlone's study.

Mary Goldie – tall, angular, elegant with a slight Canadian accent – is distinctly guarded at first. But gradually she relaxes, answers all my questions and volunteers a great deal of information. Perhaps it's my 'bedside manner' that does the trick. She tells me about her interview for the job as HRH's secretary. The one thing that neither she nor the Princess mentioned throughout the interview was salary; not until her first pay packet arrived did she know what she was to be paid. Very little, I suspect. I also suspect that the job is no pushover. She has been with the Princess for over thirty-five years and lets slip the occasional flash of resentment. 'She never thinks that I have a life of my own,' she complains at one stage.

After a tour of the house we go out to the Princess's garden: a walled area beside the Palace. As is the case with so many of these royal women of a certain generation, the garden is where they are happiest. 'She used to love nothing better,' says Miss Goldie, 'than being on her knees, weeding.' From her tone, I suspect that Mary Goldie, often forced to join in, loved nothing less.

7 October 1980

Seeing Mary Goldie yesterday reminded me of our first visit to the Princess's Kensington Palace apartment. It was in 1975 when Brian and I had come over to Britain for several months to do research: he at the Public Record Office for his official history of Kimberley and me for my *Victoria and Disraeli*. We had been invited to tea. This was served in the dining room – all blue and white to compliment HRH's celebrated collection of Delft pieces.

Although the Princess could usually follow what I said, she could never hear Brian, so he always had to bellow. A third man was expected to tea that day – a man in his early seventies, years younger than the 92-year-old Princess. 'You'll have to speak up when he comes in,' she instructed Brian. 'The poor old thing is very deaf.'

The Princess gave us an interesting bit of information that day. The last Empress of Russia, the Tsaritsa Alexandra, wife of Nicholas II, had been Princess Alice's cousin. The Princess remembered once sharing a bath with their youngest daughter, Grand Duchess Anastasia, and noting that she had 'hammer' toes. As Anna Anderson, the woman who later claimed to be the Tsar's youngest daughter, did not have hammer toes, she could not possibly be the real Grand Duchess Anastasia, maintained the Princess.

While pouring tea, Princess Alice knocked over a cup. I quickly slipped a plate under the tablecloth to protect the surface of the table from the hot tea. 'It's a trick my mother taught me,' I explained. 'Ah,' countered the Princess. 'Now I'll show you a trick *my* mother taught me.' With that she poured the spilt tea from her saucer back into her cup.

Like many old ladies, Princess Alice ate like a trencherman. 'Sheer greed,' she would say, helping herself to another slice of cake or another helping of pudding.

'See you next year,' she would always say on parting, adding cheerfully, 'if I'm still alive.'

8 October 1980

Spend the morning with the Abel Smiths at their house, Barton Lodge, in Windsor. [Lady May Abel Smith is Princess Alice's daughter.] In spite of all my protestations, I have been invited to breakfast. This has meant getting up at first light and catching an early train to Slough. Am met at Slough station by the eighty-year-old Sir Henry Abel Smith. He is a handsome old man, tall with an erect, military bearing. The drive to Barton Lodge is hair-raising. Not only is the rush-hour traffic horrendous but Sir Henry insists on turning to me, full face, whenever he says anything – which is most of the time.

The house shows that aristocratic disdain for comfort: it is bleakly furnished and freezing. We help ourselves to breakfast and sit at a vast table, across which we shout at one another.

Am very interested to meet the 74-year-old Lady May. Not only is she Queen Victoria's great-granddaughter but – through her father, the Earl of Athlone – the granddaughter of that most lovable and ebullient figure, the Duchess of Teck. Lady May was born Princess May of Teck; only after the wholescale ditching of German names during the First World War was the family name changed. She emerged from this metamorphosis with the irreproachable English title of Lady May Cambridge. Her marriage to Henry Abel Smith was not really approved of by her parents. Princess Alice thought that her only daughter could do better for herself; Abel Smith was merely one of Lord Athlone's aides-de-camp

during his years as Governor-General of South Africa. 'They hoped she'd marry the Prince of Wales [the future King Edward VIII and later Duke of Windsor] and become Queen,' Joan Lascelles once confided to me.

Like Princess Alice, Lady May is small but looks altogether more robust, less ethereal. She is a non-stop talker. Crouched over a one-bar electric fire in the drawing room after breakfast, we discuss the Princess. Lady May has by now read the rough draft of the first half of my manuscript and makes some minor corrections and suggestions. Tentatively, I raise those two delicate topics: the fact the Princess Alice is a carrier of the 'royal disease', haemophilia, and the even more embarrassing fact that HRH's late brother, Charles Edward, Duke of Coburg, was a great admirer of Hitler and was tried, after the war, for his pro-Nazi activities.

Lady May discusses both these controversial subjects with admirable breeziness. Her only brother, Viscount Trematon, had inherited haemophilia from Princess Alice and had died, in a minor car accident, in his twenties. Lady May had been afraid that she herself might be a carrier and that her only son, Richard, might inherit the disease. But, as is often the way with haemophilia, it passed him by. About her uncle, the pro-Nazi Duke of Coburg, Lady May trots out the usual line: he was not really pro-Nazi but anti-communist. 'Uncle Charlie "did some time" after the war, didn't he?' she asks airily.

Sir Henry pops his head round the door to suggest that his wife 'show Mr Aronson the Arabs'. I can't imagine what he means. 'No, Mr Aronson doesn't want to see the Arabs,' she snaps. (Like her mother before her, Lady May is the boss in this marriage.) The Arabs turn out to be their horses, in which they are both passionately interested. Lady May is right. I don't want to see the Arabs.

As the Abel Smiths are off to the races this afternoon, I leave just before lunch. On the no less hair-raising drive back to the station, Sr Henry regales me at length about Uncle Charlie's admirable anti-communism.

12 October 1980

Have lunch, and several hours of fascinating conversation, with Sir Shuldham Redfern, who had been Lord Athlone's secretary during his term as Governor-General of Canada. He tells me a very good story about Princess Alice's increasing imperiousness. The other day, as the Queen was leaving the Princess's sickroom, HRH, whose habits are spartan, snapped out an instruction. 'Turn off that heater as you go out,' she commanded. 'We only put it on because you were coming.' The Queen stooped to obey.

13 October 1980

Have invited Joan Lascelles to tea at a Kensington hotel. 'Oh dear, isn't that frightfully posh?' she protests when I suggest it. I hardly recognize her when she arrives. I am so used to seeing her in the sort of riotous floral dresses and huge white sandals that Englishwomen of her generation consider obligatory wear in hot climates. She is wearing a very boldly checked black and white cashmere coat and a smart black hat. 'They both belonged to the Princess,' she announces.

'Mrs Mellon [wife of Dr Matthew Mellon, of the wealthy Gulf Oil Mellons] gave the coat to the Princess but she's far too small to wear this sort of big check. So she passed it on to me. And she didn't want the hat any more.'

The Princess, who is by now completely bedridden, still 'looks lovely' says Joan Lascelles. She has brought me a collection of photographs, cuttings and letters concerning the Princess during her time as Chancellor of the University College of the West Indies. Not one of them, of course, is dated. 'Oh, goodness knows,' she says whenever I ask for a year.

We order tea and 'buttered toast'. We are served with a pile of soggy, barely toasted white sliced bread with the crusts left on, with butter and assorted jams in little foil-lidded plastic containers. Not posh at all.

Afterwards we stroll round to her flat in Hornton Street. She is full of complaints about the 'most *frightful* Arab landlord'. She is also convinced that the recently demolished Kensington Town Hall was knocked down on the orders of 'that *frightful* Ken Livingstone', whereas, of course, it was done by the local Tories. Her sitting room is freezing but, as she is a tough old bird, the only form of heating is the two-bar electric fire, of which only one bar is on. Her bathroom, when I go to pee, is even bleaker: a cement floor, towels like sandpaper and one of those slotted wooden bathmats we used to have at boarding school. She is dismissive of central heating and television but is very enthusiastic about her latest discovery. 'It's called "the chippy",' she explains. 'You just go and buy ready-cooked fish and chips and bring them home. *Frightfully* good.'

On getting back home I write a letter of complaint to the hotel about the ghastly tea, making a great point of the fact that it was Princess Alice's lady-in-waiting that I was entertaining.

Frome, 16 October 1980

Two significant letters in the post. One, a letter of profuse apology from the manager of that hotel in Kensington. He invites me and a guest to enjoy a meal at the hotel's expense at any time that suits me.

The other is from Clarence House. On the principle of 'nothing ventured, nothing gained', I had written to the Queen Mother's private secretary to ask if she would be prepared to give me her memories of Princess Alice. The letter informs me that 'Her Majesty Queen Elizabeth The Queen Mother will receive you in order to give you any help in her power with your book.' A date will be arranged in November. I am delighted.

17 October 1980

The first time I ever saw the Queen Mother was in 1947. In that year the British royal family – King George VI, Queen Elizabeth and their two daughters – arrived in South Africa for a ten-week-long state visit.

The object of this tour was chiefly political. Presented as a much-needed post-war holiday for the royal family and as a way of thanking South Africa for its contribution to the winning of the war, the state visit was a means whereby the

South African Prime Minister, Field Marshal Smuts, hoped to counter the growing threat of republicanism in the country. A South African election was due in 1948. Surely, reckoned Smuts, in the face of this charming family, some of the opposition to the concept of the monarchy would melt? Surely a successful royal tour would ensure that Smuts's party – the generally pro-British, anti-republican United Party – would be returned to power? About that infinitely more important question, that of Black/White relations within South Africa, Smuts tended to be somewhat vague.

The royal family, who arrived on HMS *Vanguard* in mid-February 1947, were obliged to fulfil an extraordinary round of public engagements. At times the pace was gruelling. Day after day, often in murderous heat, the visitors were on show. The so-called White Train carried them for thousands of miles: to teeming cities, placid country towns and immense African gatherings. It also brought them to remote railway sidings where a knot of mainly English-speaking people – always a minority in these rural communities – would gather to greet them. It was on one such siding that I first saw the royal family.

I had just turned seventeen and, having left school a few weeks before, was due to start at the University of Cape Town the following month. My family lived in Kirkwood, a small, dusty, sunbaked dorp (village) set in a citrus-growing area on the banks of the Sundays River. The White Train was due to stop to take on water at a railway siding called, of all things, Glenconner, about thirty miles away. So a few car loads of Kirkwood people braved the heat and dust of the dirt road to drive to Glenconner. Although I would be seeing the royal visitors the following day (my parents had been invited to a royal garden party in the nearby city, Port Elizabeth, and as my father had no interest in attending, I was to accompany my mother) this opportunity of a close-up preview was too good to miss.

Hardly more than a cindery platform, set in the treeless grey-brown veld, Glenconner was as desolate a place as one could hope to find. There we stood, about thirty of us, an oddly formal little group of country people – the women in hats and gloves and the men in suits and ties – waiting in the scorching sunshine. Eventually the immaculate ivory and gold carriages of the royal train came gliding into the station. This was followed by a flurry of activity as the equerries alighted to speak to the stationmaster. The best-looking among this group of young men was Peter Townsend, whose subsequent romance with Princess Margaret was to be one of the great royal dramas of the 1950s, and whose accent, to our South African ears, sounded extraordinarily plummy and affected.

A minute or two later, the 51-year-old King George VI alighted. Wearing a pale beige summer suit and a brown hat with its brim turned down all the way round, he looked handsome but oddly diffident. He was followed by the 46-year-old Queen, who created an entirely different impression. A consummate actress, she paused for a moment in the doorway of the carriage waving a white-gloved hand in answer to the applause which had suddenly become more spon-taneous. Although she was not really a great beauty, Queen Elizabeth was one of those women who can create an illusion of beauty. Much of this was due to her colouring – black hair, blue eyes, a skin like cream – and to her consciously feminine presentation of herself. She was dressed to the nines: in pale blue, her hat a towering confection of blue and white blossom. None of the present-day dressing down for her: even in this forlorn place and to this handful of unimportant people, she was presenting herself as a queen. The princesses, with the sort of dazzling complexions never seen in hot climates, wore simple linen dresses and headscarves.

I don't know what I, a very unworldly schoolboy, had expected the family to look like but I had certainly not been prepared for their air of glamour. At a time when the reproduction of colour photography was still comparatively rare, one was accustomed to seeing them pictured in black and white, usually in some wartime setting, inspecting bomb sites or troops or rows of nurses. Now, seen at such close quarters, they had an almost technicolour quality about them – a lustre not entirely due to who they were.

After a few words to the stationmaster, the Queen moved forward to speak to the little crowd who had by now been marshalled into a one-deep line. There then followed what can only be called an exercise in professionalism. Head characteristically tilted, she asked innumerable questions – about the weather, crops, cattle and distances – listening, in apparently rapt attention, to the boringly predictable answers. She looked, as Harold Nicolson once said of her, as though 'she had just discovered a delightful way of spending the afternoon'. If she spotted a medal pinned on to an ex-serviceman's jacket, she would ask where he had seen service. Here she would turn to the King who, unlike his wife, was making very little effort.

At times, these conversational exchanges were hilarious in

their sterility. Where, the Queen asked one ex-serviceman, had he fought? 'Italy,' he answered. 'Italy,' repeated the Queen to the King. 'Oh, Italy,' commented the King. 'Yes, Italy,' repeated the ex-serviceman. 'Um,' said the King. Only by flashing her celebrated smile and passing on could the Queen break the conversational deadlock.

With anyone who looked shabby or insignificant she would make a special effort. 'How very kind of you to come and see us,' she would say.

It was on another such railway siding that the Queen was assured by one old Boer War veteran that he could never forgive 'the English' for conquering and 'taking over' his country. 'I do sympathize with you,' she answered deftly. 'We feel exactly the same in Scotland.'

A friend, Grace Smit, and I had very cannily positioned ourselves, among a group of younger children, at the very end of the little line, so that the Queen was bound to speak to us. I no longer remember the conversation but she asked about our ages, schools and pastimes and made little jokes in a confiding, almost conspiratorial way. I was greatly impressed that she knew that Kirkwood was 'where the oranges grow'. She had obviously been briefed or had been given the information by someone further up the line.

The scene that day was full of little vignettes. The King was seen to grin when Princess Elizabeth pointed out the name of the siding: it was all a far cry from Scotland. Princess Margaret was heard to hiss 'Don't push' when her sister accidently stumbled against her. The irrepressible Kitty Muller, overwhelmed by the Queen's charm, assured her that 'you and your hubby are welcome to visit the farm at any time'.

(A similar exchange concerned a painfully inarticulate Springbok rugby player who was dancing with an almost equally inarticulate Princess Elizabeth at her twenty-first birthday ball at Government House, Cape Town. Desperately casting about for something to break the silence, he blurted out: 'I saw your Mom and Dad in town today.')

When it was finally over and the family stood framed in one of the windows as the train steamed out, the crowd broke, waveringly, into that inevitable anthem of the period, 'For they are jolly good fellows.'

But there were still two more royal encounters for us that day. On the road back home, our little convoy of cars was overtaken, in a cloud of dust, by the royal Daimlers as they raced down to Port Elizabeth to be ready, sleek and shining, to meet the White Train for the procession through the city the following morning.

And then, some miles further on, we saw the White Train drawn up. The royals were setting off on their daily walk beside the railway track. My last view was of the Queen of England, having changed into sensible shoes, striding across the parched veld in that sumptuous hat.

18 October 1980

Another, much later, encounter with the Queen Mother.

I spent most of my twenties in London, working as a designer – or commercial artist as we called them then – with the J. Walter Thompson Advertising Agency in Berkeley Square. In those days one would often come across members of the royal family by accident. I once saw the young Queen

Elizabeth II shopping at the next counter at Fortnum and Mason. On another occasion, as I was walking down Church Street, Kensington, Queen Mary emerged majestically from her Daimler, gave me a brusque nod and disappeared into an antique shop. And once, as I was walking through Belgrave Square in the pouring rain, from the office in Berkeley Square to my room off Sloane Square, a door opened and Countess Mountbatten hurried out. 'May I beg a lift under your umbrella?' she asked and, locking her arm through mine, walked us briskly to the nearby corner where she left me to enter another door.

'By accident' exactly describes my encounter with the Queen Mother. For some inexplicable reason I once had to get an ironing board from the JWT offices in Berkeley Square to Peel Street, off Kensington Church Street, where my friends, the painter Aedwyn (Ted) Darroll and his actress wife Vivienne Drummond (who was playing Helena in the original production of *Look Back in Anger*) were then living. In those days ironing boards were heavy, wooden contraptions and as I couldn't possibly afford a taxi, I was obliged to lug this board right across Hyde Park. It was late on a winter's afternoon, so quite dark.

At that time the traffic through Apsley Gate used to enter the park through the first two arches (those nearest Apsley House) and leave the park through the third arch. So, making sure that no cars were coming from the left, I crossed the first bit of road. Then, again checking that the left was clear, I stepped into the second roadway. There was a sudden roar of motorbikes, followed by a screech of brakes as a car, approaching from the *right*, shuddered to a stop just inches from me. In my fright, I dropped the ironing board. Turning to face the car, I saw that it was carrying the Queen Mother. Whereas, nowadays, Queen Elizabeth II travels through London as inconspicuously as possible, the Queen Mother, in her heyday, used to make sure that the car's interior lights were on so that she could be seen by the public. So there she sat, a radiant figure in full fig – furs, feathers, jewels – rocking with good-natured laughter at my predicament.

The explanation for all this is that the royal cars were allowed to drive either way through the central arch. I had just not taken in the fact that, as I had looked to my left, all the traffic between Apsley Gate and the Constitution Hill Arch was being held back by the police to allow the Queen Mother's car to pass through. Not until I had shamefacedly picked up the ironing board was she able to move on. Still smiling broadly, she gave me one of her ineffable waves and was swept out of sight.

19 October 1980

Had written to Lord Snowdon to tell him that my publishers would be using his photograph of Princess Alice, on her ninety-fifth birthday, on the jacket of my book, and to ask if he had anything to tell me about the Princess. Receive a polite letter today – not from Snowdon but from Buckingham Palace – to explain that it is 'Lord Snowdon's firm policy' never to contribute in any way (other than photographically) to books about members of the royal family. I assume that this is part of the divorce deal from Princess Margaret.

London, 20 October 1980

I go to Kensington Palace to see Princess Alice, Duchess of Gloucester. As usual, I am far too early (the appointment is for 6 p.m.) and spend over half an hour walking up and down Kensington Palace Gardens. At five to six I present myself to the policeman in the little sentry-like box outside the Palace. Am surprised, as always, by the apparently lax security at Kensington Palace: just a couple of cheery policemen who have one's name on a pad. Perhaps there is something more professional that I don't know about.

I ring the doorbell and am greeted by an immensely old manservant. He totters ahead of me through several large rooms, one of them a jumble of trampolines, balls, bats and crash helmets, presumably belonging to the family of Prince Richard, the young Duke of Gloucester. In a still larger room I am greeted by a young lady-in-waiting, one of the brood of Scott relations who are employed by the Duchess of Glouces-ter. A door opens, two huge black dogs come bounding in and, with cries of 'Down, Beatnik!' Princess Alice hurries into the room.

Dealing with two women called Princess Alice — one the Countess of Athlone and the other the Duchess of Gloucester — brings its problems. On the death of Prince Henry, Duke of Gloucester (he was the third son of King George V), his only surviving son inherited the title and *his* wife became the new Duchess of Gloucester. So the Dowager Duchess (the one whom I am visiting) decided to style herself Princess Alice, Duchess of Gloucester. This, in the royal hothouse

where these things still matter, caused an upheaval. Princess
Alice, Countess of Athlone, who was *born* a princess, resented
the fact that the other Alice, a commoner who had merely
married a prince, should add Princess to her own first name.
'She should have called herself Princess Henry; that is her
correct title,' Princess Alice, Countess of Athlone, once said
to me. [In later years the press and public insisted, quite
incorrectly, on referring to the Princess of Wales as 'Princess
Diana'. There is no such title.]

The Duchess – as I shall style her – is small, slender and,
at almost eighty, retains those remarkable cheekbones which,
in younger days, made her a beauty. She is simply dressed, in
a tweed skirt and a cardigan. Her movements are quick and
energetic. The lady-in-waiting sinks into one of those aston-
ishingly low curtsies, which one only ever sees in royal
households, and takes her leave. The two of us settle down
beside the fire.

The manservant offers drinks. I play safe with sherry; the
Duchess is brought what looks like a soft drink. The dog,
Beatnik, falls in love with me at first sight and buries her
head between my legs. She deeply resents my taking notes.
Every time I try to scribble something into my notebook, she
gives my hand an almighty nudge with her nose. Exasperated,
the Duchess tries to drag the dog out of the room. Beatnik
refuses to budge. Eventually I have to get up, entice the dog
into another room and slam the door on her.

The Duchess is very shy, full of nervous mannerisms.
When her hands are not being wrung, they are fluttering
about her face. I find that it is I who have to put her at her
ease, not vice versa. But she has taken considerable trouble on

my behalf, having written out a list of things to tell me. As we talk, she gradually reveals a wonderfully dry, self-deprecating sense of humour. She is especially funny about Princess Alice's inexhaustible energy. In the 1920s when the Duchess – as Lady Alice Montagu Douglas Scott – was a guest of the Athlones at Government House, Cape Town, she used to cower in her room whenever the indefatigable Princess Alice, determined on yet another set of tennis or another mammoth walk, scoured the house in search of a partner.

Reading from her list, the Duchess announces that Princess Alice is 'a great weeder'. Assuming that she pronounces 'read' as 'weed', in the same way she pronounces 'off' as 'orf', I tell her that I had, in fact, first met Princess Alice through her having read one of my books. 'No,' says the Duchess, 'I am talking about the weeding you do in a garden, not the reading you do in a book.'

As I am leaving, I tell the Duchess that I have read her own book of memoirs and of how struck I have been by her own, and the late Duke's, unquestioning sense of royal duty. This isn't flannel. What I mean, but what I don't actually say, is how impressed I have been by the way in which two such shy, inarticulate, country-loving people forced themselves to lead the sort of public life for which they had neither taste nor talent. They must have hated every minute. She is clearly touched by my remarks. 'Yes,' she says quietly, 'no one really appreciated what we did. No one ever thanked us for anything. The others got all the praise.'

The Duchess herself leads me back through all those empty, dimly lit rooms and sees me off at the front door.

London, 30 November 1980

Anne Carter and I have spent several days at Kensington Palace going through HRH's photograph albums to choose illustrations. Fascinating.

With the Princess having been bedridden for some months now, her apartment has a strangely deserted quality, as though she were already dead. None of those masses of flowers, in vases and pots, which used to fill the rooms.

But today has been greatly enlivened by the arrival of Lady May Abel Smith who talks, non-stop, about the first draft of my manuscript. She makes a great point of the fact that the Princess's hair, in younger days, was dark, not light, brown. 'My mother always said that she could wear a brown coat; none of the others could, with their blonde hair and blue eyes.' Over Lady May's shoulder, Miss Goldie gives me a quizzical look.

Having selected the photographs, we are faced with the job of getting seven huge, brass-bound albums back to the Cassell offices in Red Lion Square. It is snowing heavily. Mary Goldie offers to telephone for a taxi. Her repeated requests for the cab to come to Kensington Palace obviously baffle the person on the other end of the line. Finally, a by now desperate Miss Goldie spells out, loudly and slowly, the letters: P, A, L, A, C, E.

11 December 1980

After several postponements, I finally see Lord Harewood in his cramped office at the Coliseum. He was an aide-de-camp to the Athlones in Canada just after the war. (Lord Harewood has already put me in touch with a fellow aide-de-camp, Neville Usher, who has sent me a most valuable taped account of his time at Rideau Hall, Ottawa.) Lord Harewood is impressive to meet: easy, urbane, articulate. He looks very much the son of both his parents: the Princess Royal (King George VI's sister) and the sixth Earl of Harewood.

He has a fund of good stories and telling observations about the vice-regal couple. One interesting point concerns the Earl of Athlone's supreme self-confidence. It would simply never have occurred to the Governor-General, says Harewood, that anyone might not have liked him or approved of him or wished him well. What he means, but does not actually say, is that Lord Athlone had all the self-assurance of a not especially intelligent but 'well-born' man. Lord Harewood is very interested to hear about Mackenzie King's diaries, in which the Canadian Prime Minister has some extremely acidulous things to say about the Athlones.

I ask Lord Harewood about a story which someone has told me about him. When he was a prisoner of war in Colditz, a fellow prisoner, not realizing that he was King George VI's nephew, once asked where he lived. 'In Yorkshire,' replied Harewood. Had he ever been to London, asked his companion. 'Oh yes,' he answered, 'I have an uncle living there.'

Smilingly, Lord Harewood denies the story.

Frome, 3 January 1981

As I come in with the second round of shopping, Brian tells me that Princess Alice's death has just been announced on a mid-morning news bulletin. Although I have been expecting it, I feel saddened. During this past year, and more, I have been so intimately concerned with every aspect of her life that I feel as though I have lost a close friend. The Princess would have turned ninety-eight next month. Already she was the longest-lived member of the British royal family; if she had survived until September this year, she would have lived longer than any person born into a European royal family.

5 January 1981

Anne Carter telephones first thing. How soon can they have the finished typescript? I explain that although I have finished over three-quarters of the first rough draft, the Abel Smiths are still reading it – and having it read – and there is still a great deal of work to be done on it. Have yet to see the Queen Mother. Because of her eightieth birthday commitments, she had not been able to see me last November. And she will not be back at Clarence House until mid-February. But I promise to get the typescript to Cassell as soon as possible. (I know damn well that no matter how soon I deliver it, there will be delays in publication.)

An hour later Anne rings again. The *Daily Mail* are anxious to serialize the book or, if that is not possible, to publish an excerpt. I am very bad in this sort of situation. I feel that until the Abel Smiths have vetted the typescript, I should hold back; I feel that it would be wrong to chivvy them. And anyway, the typescript is in a messy, scrawled-on, added-to state. So we decide to leave it.

12 January 1981

A letter from Sir Henry Abel Smith, bordered in black, in answer to my letter of condolence. He writes that 'No one knows better than you do about her life of service to the Crown and to mankind . . .' In a way, I suppose that what he says is true.

London, 10 February 1981

Brian and I attend the memorial service for the Princess in St Mary Abbots, Kensington. Pleased to find that I have been allotted a special seat, in the fourth pew from the front. A stir at a side door as Princess Anne, Princess Margaret and the Duke and Duchess of Gloucester arrive. They are greeted by the Abel Smiths. Princess Anne looks less horsey than I had imagined, and Princess Margaret, in a dark fur halo hat and diamond earrings, very striking. The congregation is a sea of walking sticks, hearing aids and wheelchairs. Oddly enough, the service is an almost enjoyable affair, with plenty of the sort of rollicking hymns that HRH would have loved.

There is nothing like a morning funeral, Noël Coward

used to say, to sharpen the appetite for lunch. I have taken up the offer of a complimentary meal from the hotel which had served Joan Lascelles and me that disastrous tea, so Brian and I have a slap-up meal after the service. Even the wine is on the house.

26 February 1981

To Clarence House for my 'audience' with the Queen Mother. The road outside the house is a mass of photographers, hoping to catch a glimpse of Lady Diana Spencer who moved into Clarence House three days ago, just before the announcement of her engagement to Prince Charles.

The sentries don't even glance as I knock on the little black door in the wall. It is opened by a policeman who is, of course, expecting me. He leads me through the confusion of the Lodge to the front door of the house. My knock (for some unknown reason, I never ring bells) is immediately answered by a very old footman who almost collapses under the weight of my entirely unsuitable, Korean-made, Arctic-intended, bulkily insulated coat. Under this I am wearing a hardly more suitable tropical-weight navy-blue suit with wide lapels. I haven't got anything else. Billy [William Tallon, an old friend dating back to my earlier, more hedonistic years in London and who now enjoys the splendidly medieval-sounding title of Page of the Back Stairs] bounces up to greet me. It all seems a world away from our bedsit days.

Ahead stretches the vast hall of Clarence House, looking not unlike the foyer of a grand station hotel. I feel that I should, as my mother used to say, make myself comfortable before my momentous audience, so Billy directs me to the cloakroom. Its style is part-Edwardian, part-thirties and entirely gentleman's club: hairbrushes, clothes brushes, marble basins and brass taps.

On emerging, I am greeted by the Queen Mother's Comptroller, Captain Alastair Aird. He is in his early fifties, I imagine, with his hair neatly parted and combed in that particularly royal household way. It later emerges that he is a member of one of those families who have been associated with the monarchy for generation after generation. His father was Sir John Aird, an equerry to the Prince of Wales, afterwards King Edward VIII and then Duke of Windsor. We go into a small sitting room to the right of the front door. The walls are crowded with John Piper's watercolours of Windsor Castle, painted during the Second World War. It was on seeing these pictures, with their typically lowering John Piper skies, that King George VI commiserated with the artist for not having had better weather during his stay at the Castle. (George VI once admitted that he never knew whether the name under a portrait was that of the artist or the sitter.) Captain Aird explains that the pictures have just been reframed; but they could only afford, he says unblinkingly, to reframe half of them. I have a vision of the Queen Mother waiting for her next giro.

Suddenly we hear a tremendous barking. 'That's a sure sign Her Majesty is on her way down,' he explains. Billy pops his head round the door to say that 'Her Majesty is ready for Mr Aronson.' I follow Aird across the expanse of the hall, he opens the door of the main drawing room, bows his head and announces, 'Mr Aronson, Your Majesty.' I give Billy a quick wink and go in. Aird closes the door behind me, leaving me alone with the Queen Mother.

She is standing, huge handbag over the arm, in the middle of the room. This walk towards the royal personage is always the trickiest bit. At what stage do you nod your head? On entering the room? On shaking hands? On both occasions? She is very small, and slimmer than I had expected. At eighty, she looks about sixty-five. Instead of the sort of mauve or powder-blue chiffon I had imagined she would be wearing, she is in a dark blue satin dress, embroidered with little flowers. About her neck are ropes of pearls and she wears diamond earrings. Her figure can only be described as barrel-shaped. Her hair is wispy and festooned with little combs which she keeps tucking into place. Her teeth are discoloured. But once she begins talking, none of this matters. She says, in the most beautifully modulated voice, 'I am *delighted* to meet you. How *very* kind of you to come and see me.' It's all nonsense, of course, but from that moment on I am enslaved.

She points me, in her celebrated slow-motion way, to a little gilt chair and seats herself opposite. She sits bolt upright (I suppose that her corsets prevent anything else), head tilted. I feel that I must do the same, so there we sit, like two perched budgerigars. Her air is animated, interested; she uses her hands a great deal, often spreading them out, palms uppermost. She lays stress on certain words; a practice which, like yawning, is infectious and I find myself doing the same thing. Her charm really is exceptional without being in the least sugary. In fact, she is sharp and often sardonic. She herself has admitted to not being nearly as nice as most people imagine her to be. Having to concentrate on what she is saying, I don't really take in the room, except to appreciate that it is large, grandly furnished and filled with flowers.

She has a fund of stories about 'Aunt Alice' but not before stressing the fact that the Princess, who was in her nineties, was '*quite* a different generation' from herself, in her eighties. She describes Princess Alice as 'in many ways, a remarkable woman, full of get-up-and-go'. Too much get-up-and-go at times. On the Queen Mother's first stay at Balmoral as the newly married Duchess of York, Aunt Alice once greeted her with a rousing 'Good morning. Lovely day. Come along...' and dragged her up Lochnagar. By the time they reached the summit, the day had become distinctly less lovely and they were caught in a snowstorm. Aunt Alice found it all 'tremendous fun'.

The Queen Mother is very funny about the occasion on which the Princess, as Chancellor of the University of the West Indies during the 1960s, conferred an honorary degree on the Queen Mother. The speaker that year was the distinguished American politician, Adlai Stevenson. Having conferred the degree, Princess Alice – quite forgetting that Adlai Stevenson had still not delivered his speech – firmly announced that the ceremony was over. 'Ma'am, Ma'am, you have to call on Mr Stevenson,' hissed an anguished colleague. Instead of making the expected apology, the Princess simply covered her face with her programme and rocked with laughter. She was joined by the entire audience, including Adlai Stevenson. 'Ma'am,' he said, on finally getting to his feet, 'after your gallant effort to save me from all this...'

'My heart', the Queen Mother admits to me, 'rather sank at the sight of his great wadge of notes.' But very skilfully,

Stevenson dispensed with the greater part of them. 'Well, Mr Stevenson,' she said afterwards, 'we were together at Oxford six weeks ago, and now we meet here. Where shall it be next?'

'You name the place, Ma'am,' he answered gallantly, 'and I'll be there.'

Even during the last weeks of her life, says the Queen Mother, Princess Alice kept up her standards. Although she was bedridden, she would keep the visiting Queen Mother waiting outside her bedroom door while she 'put a little powder on her face and had her hair attended to'.

I tell the Queen Mother that I was born in South Africa. 'Ah, I know that,' she answers and, pointing across the room says, 'Look!' In a corner is a great arrangement of proteas, the South African national flower. We talk about the 1947 tour and I tell her that when I first saw her on that little railway siding, I thought she looked 'like a million dollars'. She obviously loves this. 'We so seldom hear that kind of spontaneous remark,' she says. 'It makes all our efforts seem worthwhile.'

Among her more vivid memories is of a launch trip on the Zambezi River, above and perilously close to the Victoria Falls. 'I thought that the whole dynasty was about to be swept away.'

Discussing South Africa's withdrawal from the Commonwealth, she says, 'We were so sorry to have *lost* South Africa,' for all the world as though she had mislaid it. I mutter something about the Nationalists being determined to have their republic. She then makes a curious remark. 'It's these leftists,' she says. Now the Nationalist government of South

Africa has been called many things, but never leftist. But her comment illustrates the strangely blinkered outlook of someone like the Queen Mother. So many members of the royal family view society in terms of being monarchist or anti-monarchist. The Queen Mother is clearly incapable of appreciating the forces of nationalism that might want to rid themselves of what they regard as the imperialist and monarchist yoke. Anyone who opposes the monarchy is a 'leftist'.

The Queen Mother describes the Afrikaners (who have even described themselves as 'the polecats of the world') as 'a wonderfully simple people, like the Norfolk farmers'. She even remembers a few words of Afrikaans; not bad after thirty-four years.

But everything is said in such a confiding, charming way that I simply find myself carried along. After more than an hour in her company, I wonder how and when the audience is going to end. She accomplishes this with great skill. 'Now is there anything else at all that I can help you with?' she asks, reaching down for that huge handbag (what do they keep in them?). 'Unfortunately, I've got some people coming,' she explains with a rueful smile, as though she would have loved me to stay longer. She walks towards the door, waits for me to open it and, with that famous wave of her hand, disappears upstairs.

Billy comes dashing up to say that he has never heard so much laughter coming from the room before. As we walk towards the open front door, the pack of corgis comes bounding in. 'Don't touch them,' warns Billy as I squat down to greet them. 'That one's very snappy.'

As I emerge into the street outside, the crowd of photographers surges forward. Even though I am clearly not Lady Diana, they photograph me anyway. I wonder how she is adjusting to her first days of life in the royal cage. It's somehow fitting that the next Queen Consort should be sheltering under the wing of the last Queen Consort. I only hope that she tackles the job with the same zest and professionalism.

16 March 1981

Two months ahead of schedule and by half-killing myself during the last few weeks, I deliver the completed typescript to Cassell. There's still a lot to do — notes, bibliography, editor's queries, illustration captions, index, author's note, proofs — but the main job is over. It's over eighteen months since that lunch with Gerald Pollinger. By way of celebration I treat myself to a solitary ploughman's lunch and half a pint of bitter.

PART II

'All the town clerks are *exactly* the same'

Princess Margaret on a lifetime of royal engagements

Frome, 12 December 1981

EVER SINCE THE collapse — or whatever it was — of Cassell, I have been approached by various publishers, asking if I would like to write for them. The most promising letter is from John R. Murray, son the legendary John (Jock) Murray. So today I set off for London to meet him. It all turns out to be very different from Cassell. The Cassell offices are, or were, a vast modern block in Red Lion Square; John Murray is in an old house in Albemarle Street. At Cassell I would be seen in little partitioned-off offices; at Murray's I am greeted in the splendid Byron Room. Cassell's coffee came from a machine in styrofoam mugs; at Murray's it's tea in china cups on a silver tray. Also different is that whereas, at Cassell, my publishers were always older than I was, John R. Murray is younger. I imagine that he is in his late thirties, but eager and boyish, with an undergraduate quality.

What is *exactly* the same is the lack of enthusiasm with which all my suggestions for possible future books are met. Publishers no longer seem interested in the sort of book which I used to write: my books on the Bonapartes, the Coburgs of Belgium, the Spanish Bourbons, the German Kaisers. At the end of a dispiriting session, I dredge up an idea, long ago dismissed by Cassell, for a book to be called something like *Four Kings*. It would be a dynastic history of

the British royal family, starting with the funeral of Queen
Victoria and ending with the coronation of Queen Elizabeth
II. John Murray is immediately interested but suggests that I
continue the story to the present day, up to the marriage of
Prince Charles. This would give it a wider appeal.

I don't really like writing about living people (Princess
Alice was the closest I ever got, and then only just) but can
appreciate his point. I agree and set off for Paddington
delighted, both with my new project and with my new
publisher.

Lausanne, 17 June 1982

After six months' hard work, a little holiday. We are in
Switzerland as the guests of our friend André Bothner. He
spends half the year here, the other half in Cape Town. With
his interest in both European and South African history,
André has always been very encouraging about our writing.
We are touring the country, in great and unaccustomed style,
in a hired, chauffeur-driven car.

Today we stopped at the spot near Küssnacht where
Queen Astrid, wife of King Leopold III of the Belgians, was
killed in a car crash in 1935. The King, who was driving,
lost concentration for a moment and the Queen was fatally
injured in the resulting accident. They had been a devoted
couple. It's an evocative spot, marked by a small chapel. I
had described the incident in my book *The Coburgs of Belgium*
but this is the first time that I have seen the place.

[Many years later, just after the death of Diana, Princess
of Wales, the editor of the Letters page in the *Telegraph* asked

me to write a letter about any previous royal deaths in car accidents. His page was being so swamped by letters from incensed Diana-lovers that he wanted to publish at least one letter that wasn't an attack on the press. And so, avoiding that other obvious parallel – Princess Grace of Monaco – I wrote about the car crash that killed Queen Astrid.]

Frome, 22 July 1982

This morning's post brings an invitation from Hatchard's, the booksellers, to their annual Authors of the Year party which is to be attended, this year, by the Queen. I am to be one of the 'royal' authors chosen to be presented to her. Unfortunately, the invitation has come three months too late. It has travelled, by surface mail, to our old Kommetjie address and back, again by surface mail, to Frome.

A similar thing happened a few months ago. I had an invitation to meet King Baudouin of the Belgians at some reception in Brussels; on the strength, I assume, of *The Coburgs of Belgium*. Again the invitation travelled out to South Africa and back, reaching me far too late.

So I have now stood up not one but two monarchs.

14 August 1982

I had written to Princess Margaret to ask if she would receive me in order to give me her memories and observations for my new book. Have decided to call the book *Royal Family: Years of Transition* and am angling it on the changes and adaptations made by the dynasty during this century. Today brings an invitation from the Princess to lunch with her, at Kensington Palace, one day next month.

I last saw Princess Margaret twenty-five years ago. In order to augment my meagre salary at J. Walter Thompson (in 1956 my salary, before PAYE, was £7.50 a week and I paid £4 a week for my room and kitchenette in Sloane Gardens) I had taken an evening job. I was a waiter in a newly opened restaurant off the King's Road, Chelsea, called Au Père de Nico. In time, it became very fashionable. I worked six nights a week, from 7 p.m. until about midnight. Although the wages were not especially good, the tips could be enormous, and I soon learned how to charm tips out of customers. Other advantages were that one got an evening meal and that I lived close enough to walk home. We waiters wore black jeans, blue cotton jackets and – very much of its period, this – blue, polka-dotted kerchiefs tied round the neck. The resulting look was a sort of 'King's Road French'.

One night, just as we were about to close (last orders were at 11.15 p.m.) a telephone booking was made for a party which included Princess Margaret. The manager was aghast. The restaurant, which was by now completely empty, was like a morgue. He frantically raked in whatever friends lived nearby and ordered his more presentable-looking waiters to change into their street clothes. (In those days even the artists at JWT wore suits.) By the time the Princess's party arrived, the place was filled with apparently animated diners.

Princess Margaret, then aged twenty-five, was regarded as one of the most glamorous figures on the world stage; arguably the most eligible woman in the world. She certainly looked stunning that night, in a glittery white evening dress, smoking cigarette after cigarette through a long black holder. But our admiration soon palled as we sat, nursing our cups of coffee (which was all that the manager allowed us) and keeping up bright conversation for almost two hours until the Princess and her party were ready to leave. I can't imagine anyone allowing themselves to be put through this sort of charade, unpaid, today. But it all helped fortify the unreal, rose-coloured view of the world then enjoyed by members of the royal family.

And now here I am, twenty-five years later, being invited to lunch with the Princess. My sisters – Peggy Manby from Kent, and Jean Pitchford who, with her husband Peter, is on her way back to South Africa from the States – are staying with us for a few days. We discuss what I should wear for the lunch. It doesn't take much discussion as I have only two suits. They reject the navy-blue one which I wore to see the Queen Mother ('It looks funny,' says Peggy) and settle for the Prince of Wales check. It does look more dashing. Not, I suppose, that Princess Margaret will notice. On the other hand, she might.

29 September 1982

A fraught day. I am due at Kensington Palace at one o'clock for my lunch with Princess Margaret. A train leaves Westbury station [five miles from Frome] just after nine-thirty and is due at Paddington a few minutes after eleven. That should have given me plenty of time to get to the Palace by one. As I leave home it starts pouring with rain so I go back in to get my umbrella. Opening it in the doorway I break one of the spokes which tears through the fabric. Our only other umbrella is in an even worse state. So I bandage up the spoke with a strip of pink elastoplast. I arrive at Westbury to discover that the train is an hour late. I reach Paddington just before twelve-thirty and decide that the tube will be quicker than a taxi. Have the usual nightmare journey on the Circle Line – doors not closing, stopping forever at stations, crawling along at snail's pace – and have to run all the way, in streaming rain, from High Street Kensington to the Palace. I knock on Princess Margaret's door just as the clock in the tower is striking one.

The butler suggest that we leave my umbrella open as it's so wet. A slight lift of one eyebrow makes his opinion of my wretched bit of elastoplast quite clear. I am wearing a short navy coat with a zip and in my anxiety to get the coat off as quickly as possible, I catch the zip on the lining at mid-chest. Nothing budges it. The butler and I both tug away but it simply will not shift. 'It's already four minutes past one,' he mutters. 'Her Royal Highness doesn't like to be kept waiting.' Eventually I have to hold up my arms and bend over as he works the coat up over my head. Hair all over the place I am led into the drawing room. The Princess is sitting at her desk in the far corner. She gets up, takes off her heavily framed glasses and stands watching me as I cross the vastness of the room towards her. All I need, I think, is to fall flat on my face before reaching her. I don't.

Princess Margaret is still, at fifty-two, very attractive. Her air is theatrical and sophisticated; her voice drawling and ginny – although, actually, it's whisky. Her hair is dyed a deep, glossy auburn; her lipstick is very bright. She is small, with a big bust that gives her a somewhat top-heavy look. She is badly dressed, in a black dress patterned in yellow and green squares and is wearing white, high-heeled, platform-soled sandals which, because her legs are so thin, give her a Minnie Mouse look. She wears a great deal of jewellery.

Next to the blazing fire (is this allowed in central London these days?) stands a trolley, laden with bottles. She asks what I would like to drink (she already has one) and I ask for a little Cinzano. 'Just that?' she asks. 'Wouldn't you like a drop of gin in it?'

'No thanks,' I answer. 'If I drink too much I tend to get out of hand.'

'How *very* interesting,' says the Princess.

To get things started I ask how much she remembers of the state visit to South Africa in 1947. 'Every *minute* of it,' she says in her emphatic fashion. The tour afforded her two of the most magnificent natural sights she has ever seen: the Drakensberg mountains and the Victoria Falls.

I had been asked to send the Princess a list of questions beforehand and, in businesslike fashion, she gets this out, puts on her glasses and begins to go through them. She is very articulate and often very funny in a dry, sardonic way. She displays an understandable world-weariness when talking about her decades in public life. 'All the town clerks are *exactly* the same; all the students at Keele [the university of which she is chancellor] have just discovered Marx.' Her frankness is sometimes astonishing ('A ghastly boy. I never really liked him,' she says of one close relation) but any hint of overfamiliarity on my part is met with an icy stare. I find her disconcerting; very approachable one moment, very imperious the next. She is very much a king's daughter, a queen's sister.

Her views can be wonderfully idiosyncratic. We discuss the aboliton of the royal presentation parties at which the Season's debutantes would be presented to the monarch, and which, in the more egalitarian atmosphere of post-Second World War Britain, had become an anachronism. 'We had to stop them,' she explains, 'every *tart* in London was being presented.' In other words, the presentation parties had not been abolished because they had become too exclusive, but because they were no longer exclusive enough.

Lunch is not without its diversions. I plunge my fork into the first course – a Scotch egg – which promptly flies off the plate. The Princess turns her head away as I do the only thing I can: lift it back on to my plate with my fingers. When, during the main course – a chicken curry – the Princess thumps the poppadom on her side plate, scattering pieces all over the floor, I instinctively leap to my feet and start gathering them up. 'Don't do that,' she says and, nodding towards the butler, adds, 'let him do it. That's what he's here for.' While I munch merrily away, she picks at her food, eating almost nothing. The same can't be said about her drinking. She drinks and smokes resolutely throughout the meal. She uses a long holder into which she inserts a filter; by the end of the meal the ashtray is overflowing. She has a way of running her tongue over her teeth, and at one point during the meal she takes out a compact and re-applies her bright red lipstick.

The Princess is very interesting about her grandmother,

Queen Mary. 'She was absolutely terrifying. She didn't really like children and made no sort of effort with them.' As the Princess matured, however, she came to appreciate that the old Queen was not nearly the ogre of her childhood imaginings. 'Queen Mary was one of those women who prefer male company. Although my mother always said that she was a wonderful mother-in-law, Queen Mary didn't really like other women. She would put herself out tremendously for men, and could be utterly charming. After the war, when some of my men friends were put next to Queen Mary at dinner, they would be terrified at the prospect. But they came away enchanted. "She was so interesting," they would say. "And she was so interested in what we had to say." '

I ask the Princess about her relationship with that royal black sheep, the late Duke of Windsor. Had she seen much of him after his abdication? 'Only at funerals,' she drawls, And that even blacker sheep, the Duchess of Windsor? 'I once saw her in a hotel in New York. She looked so gloomy that I sent her a signed photograph of myself, just to cheer her up.' I hope, but don't say, that the Duchess was duly cheered. (There is an apocryphal story that while attending the Duke of Windsor's burial at Frogmore at Windsor, the Duchess, drugged and disorientated, slipped her arm through Princess Margaret's and asked, 'Having a good time, honey?' I don't bring this up either.)

The Princess is very bitter about the press. Like so many royals, she is inclined to blame the public reception of herself – that she is haughty, idle and self-indulgent – on misrepresentation by journalists. She is the first member of the royal family to have lived her life in the full glare of the media spotlight. Perhaps if she had led a less newsworthy, less rackety life, she would have had less cause to complain.

Towards the end of the meal, I am treated to a couple of her celebrated mimicries: one American, the other a sort of stage cockney. We are discussing Sir Harold Acton, in whose Florentine home she often spends holidays, when – for no apparent reason – she suddenly refers to him, as 'Sir 'Arold'. [I am reminded of the story about the biographer, Michael Holroyd, who, on hearing what he took to be the Princess's impersonation of the Goon character, Bluebottle, obligingly doubled up with laughter. Unfortunately, she had been speaking in her normal voice.]

I am uncharacteristically ill at ease throughout our meeting. I don't exactly know why. She is helpful enough and friendly enough but I find her unsympathetic, daunting, edgy. I suppose that it's not easy for her either: everything she says can so easily be twisted.

On leaving – and she sees me out to her front door herself – I offer to send her a gift copy of my Princess Alice book.

'I've got it,' she says. 'We've *all* got it.'

2 October 1982

A call late last night from an American serviceman stationed in Germany. (How do these people get my number?) Can I tell him if King Christian IX of Denmark ever fathered an illegitimate child? Why does he want to know? Because he is sure that his own, Danish-born, father is this illegitimate child. What makes him so sure? Because his father always referred to *his* daughter – the GI's sister – as 'my little princess'.

I explain that as King Christian IX died in 1906 at the age of almost ninety, it is highly unlikely. Could it, he persists, have been some other king? I say that I really don't know. Could I possibly research the matter for him? Together, he and I could make 'a fortune' out of a book on the subject. I tell him, as I always do in these situations, that I am extremely busy but that if I ever come across anything I will let him know. He gives me his address and swears me to secrecy. If the truth were ever to come out, he explains (having by now forgotten that we are about to make our fortunes by publishing a book about it) there would be 'a revolution' in Denmark.

18 November 1982

Just back from a few days in London where I've been in and out of various palaces interviewing men with sonorous titles: Lieutenant-Colonel Sir John Johnston, Comptroller the Lord Chamberlain's office at St James's Palace; Lieutenant-Colonel Sir Simon Bland, Private Secretary to the Duke of Gloucester, and Lord Napier and Ettrick, Private Secretary to Princess Margaret, at Kensington Palace.

Face-to, they all turn out to be approachable, unassuming men, ready to give me whatever help they can. Which isn't, frankly, very much; or rather, not much more than I already know. But here and there I unearth an interesting bit of information. Sir John Johnston explains that whereas, in King George V's day, the monarch would have known every guest at a royal garden party, these days Queen Elizabeth II doesn't know a soul. Sir Simon Bland tells me that after the late Duke of Gloucester suffered the stroke which left him unable to speak or respond to conversation, the Duchess (now Princess Alice, Duchess of Gloucester) insisted that he be dressed every day and be treated as though he were still a fully involved member of the family. Lord Napier — the least discreet of these courtiers (he wears white socks with his dark suit) — has a great deal to tell me about the late Duke's drinking habits.

11 December 1982

A letter from Victor Chapman, the Queen's Assistant Press Secretary, in answer to my request for an interview with Prince Charles. He will show the Prince my letter at his next Programme Meeting, on 14 December, and will let me have an answer as soon as possible.

14 December 1982

Have been told by Mrs Bane, the head librarian in Frome, that there is an old man living in the town who used to know Prince Felix Yusupov, the man who murdered Rasputin. This is too good an opportunity to miss so I arrange to go and see him. He is over eighty, very sprightly, and lives in one of a complex of retirement cottages.

He met Yusupov in the United States and obviously got to know him quite well. He can tell me nothing, of course, about Rasputin's murder but is full of information about

Yusupov himself. Very tentatively, because he is an old man, I bring up the question of Yusupov's homosexuality. I needn't have been so hesitant. 'Fucked anything that moved,' he announces briskly. 'He'd make a hole in a melon and fuck that if there wasn't anything else.'

30 December 1982

A letter from Victor Chapman, addressing me as 'Dear Theo', (we have never met) to say that Prince Charles has agreed to see me. The interview will take place on Thursday 17 February at Kensington Palace. Chapman wants me to telephone him to discuss 'further details'.

10 January 1983

The 'further details' mentioned by Victor Chapman turn out to be a proposed meeting with all three of the Queen's Press Secretaries in order to discuss my forthcoming interview with Prince Charles. So today I go up to Buckingham Palace. The policeman at the gate is expecting me; so is the man who opens the door. And so, obviously, is a young liveried footman who comes dashing up with a copy of my *Princess Alice* for signing.

Victor Chapman is a Canadian, and so not your run-of-the-mill royal functionary. He is friendly and expansive. He introduces me to the Queen's Press Secretary, Michael Shea and to the other Assistant Press Secretary, John Haslam. In the end, what all their polite circumlocution – about checking certain facts, etc. – boils down to is that they want to see what I have written about Princes Charles before it is incorporated into the typescript. I had half expected this, anyway, although none of the other royals have ever asked to be shown anything before publication.

It is arranged that I will present myself at Buckingham Palace at eleven on the morning of the interview and that John Haslam will take me to Kensington Palace to meet the Prince.

London, 17 February 1983

Arrive at Buckingham Palace for my appointment with John Haslam. Unlike Chapman, Haslam is the quintessential royal servant: friendly enough but dry and discreet. He drives me to Kensington Palace. The feel of the Prince's apartment is quite different from the other royal homes: airier, brighter; the combined taste, I imagine, of the Princess of Wales and her South-African-born decorator, Dudley Poplack. We are greeted by an enormously fat, enormously camp butler. Between them, he and Haslam can't decide who is to take me up to the Prince. 'I haven't been fought over for *years*,' I say. The butler hoots; even Haslam manages a wintry smile.

Prince Charles receives me in his study. He is shorter than I imagined, and better-looking. He has a scar high up on one cheek. His clothes have improved since his marriage; they are more stylish, less stodgy. I note the celebrated mannerisms as he greets me: the plucking at his top-pocket handkerchief, the fiddling with his tie, the shooting of his cuffs. He has just been sitting for his portrait so we talk about painting. I tell him that I spent four years at the Michaelis School of

Art at the University of Cape Town and then twelve years as a designer with J. Walter Thompson. He shows me one of his watercolours and I pass on a piece of – I suppose obvious – advice given to me years ago: about never being afraid of the blank white watercolour paper.

He asks why I am writing the book. This throws me. I can't think of a single valid reason; or, at least, any reason that would satisfactorily answer his question. (I should be used to the question by now: it is invariably the first question asked by radio or television interviewers.) I can't say for the money, or because writing is my job, or because the publishers preferred it to my other suggestions. I blurt out that, having dealt with other royal dynasties, I felt that it was time to examine the way in which the British monarchy had adapted itself and so proved more durable than some of the others. This is, in fact, the theme of the book. My answer seems to satisfy him.

I ask about his earliest memories. He has only one memory of his grandfather, King George VI, who died when he was three. This is of the King's watch chain as he sat on his knee. But he feels, says the Prince, a great affinity with his late grandfather. I suspect that this is due to Prince Charles's deep affection for the Queen Mother. Or perhaps there's something in King George VI's diffidence which appeals to him. He was certainly a very different man from Prince Charles's own extrovert and self-assured father, Prince Philip.

His only memory of his mother's coronation is of the 'gunge' (he is full of such old-fashioned words) with which his hair was plastered down for the occasion. He remembers being taken for drives by his great-grandmother, Queen Mary, in her old Daimler in Richmond Park, when she would sit, stiff-backed and unsmiling, never uttering a word.

Clearly, his best days were at Cambridge. If he were not the Prince of Wales, he admits, he would happily go back to Cambridge to study constitutional history. It seems an odd remark for a recently married man to make.

I tell him that I have already seen Princess Margaret for my book. Do I imagine a slight curling of his lip? 'Oh really,' he says, 'was *she* any help?'

He comes across as very serious-minded, very conscious of his obligations to the monarchy and the country. I cannot imagine any of the sons of King George V being as articulate as this. He talks about his theories of modern kingship. He would like, he says somewhat fancifully, to be a sort of medieval king, a 'king for all the people'. He strikes me as being very alive to the vulnerability of his position. He seems uneasy about his inherited wealth, his unearned privileges, his unreal existence, his personal fallibility. He knows that his job is only what he makes of it; that he must work hard to prove that he is relevant to these last decades of the twentieth century.

At times he appears quite astute; at others extraordinarily naive. He was very impressed, he tells me, by the national coming-together, the sort of nationwide consensus at the time of his wedding. Why couldn't it always be like that? As though all that were needed to keep the nation loyal, happy and united was a series of royal marriages.

He is interesting about the press. He feels that the Palace should be more co-operative. There is a lot of complaint about press intrusion, he argues, but it would be more

worrying if the newspapers were to stop showing an interest
in the doings of the royal family. The fact that the press
remained interested showed that the monarchy was still a
living, thriving institution. 'My wife', he says, 'is only gradually adjusting' to journalistic pressures. He also mentions his
infant son, Prince William. He thinks that the Prince should
become more closely concerned, at an earlier age, with the
day-to-day business of the monarchy. 'I hope that someone
reminds me of this in about twenty years' time,' he adds
wryly.

An indication that the interview is going well is provided
halfway through. An equerry comes in to announce that there
is someone to see the Prince. 'I'm afraid I'm busy at the
moment,' says Prince Charles. This is clearly a ploy; a way to
get rid of me if necessary. Happily, it is not necessary and I
remain for the allotted hour and a half.

As we part, the Prince wishes me good luck with the book
and I wish him good luck with his painting.

'What I really need is time,' he sighs. 'I never have enough
time.' I simply don't believe this. He may not know it but he
has a damn sight more free time than the rest of us.

2 March 1983

John Haslam returns the piece I have written about Prince
Charles. There is only one suggested correction. Where I say
that the Prince is allowed access to state papers, Haslam asks
me to change it to read 'some state papers'.

10 March 1983

To Clarence House to see the Queen Mother for *Royal Family: Years of Transition*. She is rather more grandly dressed on this occasion, in turquoise silk with floating panels. I tend not to notice jewellery (and know nothing about it) but would have to have been blind not to take in today's array: ropes of pearls, diamond earrings, an elaborate, fist-sized diamond brooch pinned high on her left shoulder. The room is filled with flowers. I assume that she is due to host a lunch party.

As before, she has done her homework. 'I can't *believe* it's two years since you last came to see me,' she says. I am, as I am meant to be, duly flattered. She asks if I have driven up from the West Country. I explain that I always drive as far as Osterley, leave the car there and take the tube into London. 'You're very wise,' she says. 'It's so difficult to find parking in London these days.' I have visions of the royal Daimler, cruising desperately around the West End.

I ask if I can put some questions to her. 'Isn't that the object of the exercise?' she asks wryly. She is dismissive of her own role in the gradual modernization of the monarchy. 'We never consciously set out to change things; we never said "Let's change this or introduce that." Things just evolved.' Yet it was in no small measure due to her warmth and spontaneity, after the stiffness of George V and Queen Mary, that the monarchy became more popular.

She tells me an amusing story about the 1939 state visit to Canada. The royal train once stopped at a little station where they were greeted by the local mayor. The King, noticing that the mayor wasn't wearing a chain of office, asked if he had a mayoral chain. 'Oh yes, I have,' answered the mayor. 'But I notice you're not wearing it,' remarked the King. 'No,' explained the mayor, 'I only wear it on *special* occasions.' For years after that, whenever the royal family members were dressed for some gala function, they would ask each other 'Is this a *special* occasion?'

Now and then she will come out with a quaintly dated phrase. By the end of the Second World War, she was 'absolutely whacked'; an East African safari in the 1920s was 'simply heaven'.

Two especially interesting points emerge from the wealth of information and observation. She is, she tells me, extremely shy. Having been shy as a girl, she had always imagined that this shyness would disappear as she grew older. But it never has. She dreads speaking in public and still has to steel herself to face strangers. I find this almost impossible to believe about a person whose ease of manner has become legendary. Can only assume that she has made full use of her unyielding sense of vocation to overcome this handicap.

The other point concerns her relationship with her late husband, King George VI. Without actually saying so, she is clearly anxious to dispel the widespread notion that she was the stronger character, the power behind the throne. She uses expressions like 'I had to ask the King about that...' and 'The King decided that it would be best...' (I believe that when the historian John Wheeler-Bennett wrote the official biography of King George VI, the Queen Mother asked him to tone down the many references to the importance of her role in the King's life.) Am not entirely convinced by this show of wifely submissiveness. If the Queen did not dominate her more diffident husband, she certainly bolstered him to an extraordinary degree. One comes away from the Queen Mother with the clear impression that for all her celebrated charm and joie de vivre, she is a woman with a core of steel.

Her affection for and admiration of her eldest grandson, the Prince of Wales, is very apparent. When I tell her that I have already interviewed him, she says, 'Yes, he's the one to see. He's got all the ideas.' She refers to him as 'a darling'.

'Wherever you go in the world,' she says to me at one point during our discussion, 'you will always find a wonderful Scotswoman doing a wonderful job of work.' I think, but don't say, that this pretty well sums up her own contribution to the monarchy.

Frome, 25 March 1983

To Lord Weidenfeld's party last night for the launching of Christopher Warwick's biography of Princess Margaret; HRH was due to attend. I suspect that Warwick has been employed to put the Princess's side of the story in her divorce from Lord Snowdon.

Consternation as we are getting into our seldom-worn dinner jackets. Brian discovers six moth holes in the inner thigh, just below the crotch. Through them, his white flesh shines like so many stars. In the little time we have left, there is only one thing to do. We smear black shoe polish on to his leg. If he remembers to keep his legs together and his jacket buttoned all should be well.

Problem solved, or at least shelved, we present ourselves at

Lord Weidenfeld's house on the Chelsea Embankment. Know no one there other than Elizabeth Longford and Hugo Vickers. Meet Christopher Warwick for the first time.

The Princess, in wide-skirted brown taffeta, is greeted by a flurry of half-hearted curtsies. At one stage I find myself alone with her. I am astonished, not only because she remembers me, but because she knows that I have recently seen the Queen Mother. Do they tell each other this sort of thing? 'I hear you visited my mother last week,' she says. That established, there seems to be nothing more to say. She asks no questions; I feel that I shouldn't ask any questions. She complains about the, admittedly harsh, overhead lighting and, shielding her eyes with her hand, peers about in comic fashion. I am saved by the arrival of a veteran woman broadcaster, who has obviously been dying to be introduced. In a flood, she explains how she has reported on every stage of the Princess's life, from the time of the Coronation of 1937. HRH cuts her short. 'Are you one of those terrible journalists', she asks, 'always telling lies about us?' The poor woman is dumbfounded and, I imagine, heartily disillusioned. She slinks away.

Food is set out on a buffet table and we are told to help ourselves. Of course, no one moves. Finally, because I am famished, I suggest to the woman beside me that we each take a plate and get started. At once, a man rushes up to grab the still-empty plates out of our hands. 'Those plates are for the Princess's party,' he hisses. So we have to content ourselves with a couple of lesser plates.

As not even a princess can break my bed-before-midnight rule, we slip away. [Have since heard that we missed the highlight of the evening. The Earl of Dudley had written a satirical poem about Princess Margaret's bête noir, Princess Michael of Kent. As his recitation progressed and the verses became increasingly scurrilous, Lord Dudley wondered if he dare continue. But the Princess's appreciative 'Wow!' gave him all the encouragement he needed. Inevitably, reports of the poem, and of Princess Margaret's enthusiastic reaction, got back to Princess Michael.]

Paris, 20 June 1983

With the typescript of *Royal Family: Years of Transition* safely delivered to John Murray, we are spending a month in Paris staying in the apartment belonging to my niece, Sue Manby. She is in London. I've never known heat like this; even in the evenings, when we venture out to eat, the streets are like a furnace.

Today brings the proof of the book jacket. Very good. It's red with gold lettering; in the centre is a picture of the young King George VI with Princess Elizabeth, both in profile.

Publication is set for late October in Britain, and some time next spring in the States.

Frome, 20 October 1983

Publication day (among other things, a good display in Hatchard's window) brings another treat. I get home from London to find Brian in a state of high excitement. We have been offered a free cruise to Cape Town. A shipping line is hoping to reintroduce a regular passenger service between Britain and South Africa and, in addition to various journalists, a few so-called celebrities with British and South African links are being invited to sail on the curiously named *World Renaissance* next month. Jock [Jock Webster, a lifelong friend who works for the South African Tourist Board in London] will also be on board. Am delighted to hear that the ship will call at the island of St Helena.

We don't even have to sing for our supper; all we are asked to do is to 'speak well' of them. I'm ready to speak as well of them as I can.

St Helena, 6 December 1983

This is my third visit to St Helena. I was first here in 1951, when Ted Darroll and I, having just graduated from the University of Cape Town, were on our way to spend a year in Britain. Our ship called in at St Helena for the day. Am ashamed to say that I didn't visit Napoleon's house (Longwood) or grave on that occasion. For one thing, I wasn't particularly interested in Napoleon and, for another, we had to watch every penny and couldn't afford the taxi fare to Longwood.

My second visit, in 1957, was very different. By then I was extremely interested in Napoleon. In fact, I was obsessed by the whole Napoleonic saga. One aspect of the Bonaparte story that particularly interested me was a curious parallel in the lives of the four leading members of the dynasty: Napoleon I, his son the King of Rome, Napoleon III and his son the Prince Imperial. All four men died in exile (the fathers in maturity, the sons in youth) and all four were buried twice.

The more I read about these four characters, the more determined I became to visit the various places connected with their deaths: their places of exile and their first and second places of burial.

So, in September 1956, having saved whatever money I could from my night job as a waiter, I took six months' leave of absence from J. Walter Thompson and, putting a pack on my back, embarked on a great Napoleonic pilgrimage. I visited Paris for the second tombs of Napoleon I and his son; Vienna for the place where the King of Rome died and was first buried; Zululand in South Africa, where the Prince Imperial was killed; St Helena where Napoleon I died and was first buried; Chiselhurst in Kent where Napoleon III and the Prince Imperial were first buried; and Farnborough in Hampshire to where the bodies of Napoleon III and his son were later moved. I travelled alone, mainly by hitch-hiking (in those days it was possible to hitch-hike as I did almost all the way down British Africa) and was quite shameless about doing whatever was necessary to get myself a meal and a bed for the night. (Luckily, I was already in Khartoum when the Suez War broke out.) I spent a few weeks with my parents in South Africa and then sailed back, via St Helena, to Britain.

My plan was to write a first-person account of my great journey: a sort of travel-cum-history book. And this is what, on my return to Britain, I did. But no publisher was interested. Nor were they interested in two further manuscripts — both on different aspects of the Bonaparte story.

For several years these three unpublished manuscripts did the rounds until an American publisher asked Gerald Pollinger, my British agent, whether he knew of anyone who could write a family history of the Bonapartes, from the birth of Napoleon until the present day. Gerald showed him my three typescripts and, on the strength of these, he commissioned what was to become my first published book: *The Golden Bees: The Story of the Bonapartes*. The book – helped by a review in *Time* magazine and by being chosen as a Book of the Year by the *New York Times* – was a considerable success and was translated into several languages. I was able to give up advertising and become a full-time writer, which I have been ever since.

But, all in all, it took almost eight years from the time I made my pilgrimage until *The Golden Bees* was published. Yet I was invariably described as 'an overnight success'.

On my 1957 visit (while sailing back to Britain) I spent two days and a night on St Helena: the ship needed some repairs. This gave me plenty of opportunity to see, not only Longwood House and Napoleon's grave, but the whole island.

This third visit is a night-time one. The most frightening storms have delayed the *World Renaissance* which means that it is already sunset by the time we drop anchor off the island. We are rowed ashore and take a taxi to Longwood. John Murray has given me a letter to deliver to another of his authors: Gilbert Martineau. Martineau is one of the great personalities of the South Atlantic. He is the French Consul on St Helena and, as Longwood House and Napoleon's grave belong to France, he acts as curator, a sort of keeper of the flame. He has been on the island for over thirty years. Martineau lives just behind Longwood House, in the quarters that were once occupied by members of the Emperor's bickering and dispirited entourage.

I knock on his door and hand him the letter. He thanks me very brusquely and is about to close the door in my face when I hurriedly explain that I am not — as I assume he thinks — a member of the ship's crew, but a fellow Murray author. From then on he is all affability; in fact, he talks without drawing breath, like a man who has been longing for conversation. It must be a lonely life for him here: St Helena has no airport and ships call very infrequently. The occasional nightmare for him is when the little capital, Jamestown, is filled with drunken French sailors ashore for a night.

He gives Brian, Jock and me a guided tour of the house. It is more fully furnished than when I was last here, twenty-five years ago. He tells us about an extraordinary American woman who arrived on the island a few months ago, posing as some sort of reincarnation of the Empress Josephine. For weeks she hung about Longwood, making a pest of herself until Martineau was obliged to forbid her entry to the house and grounds.

I find these little rooms at Longwood very moving. When one thinks of the great palaces of the Tuileries, Saint Cloud, Fontainebleau and Compiègne, it seems extraordinary that this towering historical figure should have ended his days in this modest villa. His grave is equally moving. For some twenty years, until it was moved to Paris, Napoleon's body lay under this unmarked stone, with its railed surround, in Geranium Valley. Yet one feels closer to the real Napoleon here than one does looking down on his massive sarcophagus under the dome of Les Invalides in Paris.

My only regret, on this second visit, is that Brian can't see the island by daylight. It's a fascinating place.

Cape Town, 16 December 1983

We are staying with fellow writer Joy Collier in Oranjezicht on the lower slopes of Table Mountain: a spectacular setting. A couple of days after our arrival we heard that Mary Renault had died and the next day we were asked, by her lifelong companion, Julie Mullard, to be pall-bearers at her funeral in St George's Cathedral. In the early days we were very friendly with Mary and Julie, always having Christmas dinner with them in their wonderful house on the beach. After reading my *The Fall of the Third Napoleon*, Mary gave me a Staffordshire figure of Napoleon III. When you shake it, it rattles. 'Those are the gallstones that killed him,' said Mary, who used to be a nurse. But, politically, we did not see eye to eye. Mary found our views too liberal, we thought hers too reactionary. In fact, by the time we left South Africa, four years ago, we were not on speaking terms. This often happens in the politically charged atmosphere of this country. But, of course, we were only too pleased to do this for Julie.

The service yesterday was very simple. The congregation was made up of the sort of people with whom Mary, who was intensely shy, felt most at ease: actors, dancers and members of the Cape Town PEN Club, of which Mary had been president.

Port Alfred, 23 December 1983

We are spending Christmas with my Pitchford relations: my sister Jean and her husband Peter, and their daughter Liz, now married to Graham Grant. Wonderfully relaxing, with miles and miles of almost deserted beaches to walk along. On New Year's Eve, Liz and Graham will give us the 800-mile long lift to Johannesburg, from where we catch our plane home – a daylight flight on Sabena.

John Murray telephones today (a great event here, this international call) to say that he has just heard that my American publishers intend taking me to the States for a promotional tour in the spring.

Frome, 14 January 1984

A member of the ship's company on the *World Renaissance*, on finding out who I was, asked me to do him a favour. His mother had once worked for the Duke and Duchess of York – the future King George VI and Queen Elizabeth. She had had to leave their service very suddenly and he was anxious to know when exactly this had happened. I promised to do what I could. So, on getting back home, I wrote to Alastair Aird, the Queen Mother's Comptroller, to ask if he could find out something about the woman.

A letter back today to say that his extensive enquiries, from the Queen Mother down, reveal nothing. No one has heard of her. Write to my enquirer to tell him this.

What the man is trying to prove, I imagine, is that his

mother was forced to leave royal service because she had become pregnant by the Duke of York, and that he is the illegitimate son of the future King George VI and half-brother to Queen Elizabeth II. It's odd how the very people who would, in the ordinary way, do everything to hide their illegitimacy, are only too anxious to proclaim it if there is a chance that their parentage might be royal.

I daresay the man's mother was impregnated by some footman.

New York, 4 June 1984

We are staying with Wayne (Will) Swift and Ralph Blair in their apartment on Park Avenue for a few days before moving on to the Barbizon Plaza on Monday, when the book tour begins in earnest. Wayne has arranged for me to address the English Speaking Union on 'Writing Royal Biography'. So this evening I do my stuff. Am slightly apprehensive, not knowing how much an American audience differs from a British.

But I'm not anything like as apprehensive as when I first spoke in public. This was in 1965, soon after *The Golden Bees* was published. Brian and I were then living in Swaziland, a British Protectorate wedged between South Africa and Mozambique. We had gone there for two reasons: one, as a break from the iniquities of the apartheid regime in South Africa and two, to enable me to qualify for a British passport, with a view to eventually moving to Britain permanently. It would be as well for both Brian and me to have British passports.

One day, as I was collecting our post in the little capital,

Mbabane, a woman asked me if I was 'the author'. On hearing that I was, she asked if I would come and give a talk to the members of the Ladies Church Guild of Manzini – Swaziland's other little town. I refused. I explained that I had never spoken in public before, that I was far too nervous and that I would probably make a fool of myself. I could only do it, I added jokingly, if I were drunk. Off she went.

A few days later she drove up to the remote cottage where we then lived (no electricity, no telephone) and asked me to reconsider. The ladies of the Church Guild of Manzini had had a meeting and had discussed ways in which they could get me to change my mind. In the end they had come up with what they hoped would be the perfect solution. It was this. Instead of me speaking to them in the church hall as usual, what they would do was to take a room at the George Hotel. There would be drinks before the speech; there would be drinks after the speech; and that if I felt like having a drink during the speech, that would be in order.

I explained that I wasn't an alcoholic and that tea would do very well. I went and, in the end, didn't actually disgrace myself. Ever since then, I've been a very active public speaker. So I've always had a soft spot for the Ladies Church Guild of Manzini.

Tonight, at the English Speaking Union, things go very well. The American audience laughs in exactly the same places as a British one. After the talk, I am besieged and sign lots of books. I am particularly struck by the way in which – to these ex-pats and Anglophiles – the royal family is synonymous with Britain, in a way it never seems to be at home. Time and again I am told that the royal family is 'just too wonderful', as though it were some coherent mass, and not merely a collection of widely differing family members, some admirable, some appalling.

Brian is trapped by some earnest would-be woman writer who lays down the law on the writing of biography, regardless of the fact that he is the author of ten published books.

8 June 1984

A telephone call to our room at the Barbizon Plaza from Los Angeles, where I am to appear on several TV shows, including a breakfast one. Have had to send a batch of photographs of various royals for use on this show. A girl with a Mexican-sounding name is ringing to identify these people. The only ones she recognizes are the Queen, 'Andy' and, of course, 'Lady Di'.

'There's an old lady in like a fancy hat,' she says. 'Who's that?'

'That's the Queen Mother.'

'The Queen's mother,' she says.

'No, the Queen Mother,' I insist. 'She is the Queen's mother but is always known as the Queen Mother. She was once Queen.'

'Gee,' she says, 'where was she Queen of?'

She then wants to know who 'the kind of goofy-looking guy with the big ears' is.

'Prince Charles, the Prince of Wales.'

'Of *Wales*? Isn't he the Prince of England?'

This also I explain to her.

'Then there's like an old man with a beard, in like robes and a crown.'

'That's King George V.'

'Who's he?'

'Well, he was the present Queen's grandfather.'

'Oh. Did you interview him for your book?'

I have this sudden vision of myself interviewing a proud old codger, sitting on a rocking chair on the front porch, whose clever granddaughter has made it to queen. I explain that he died almost fifty years ago and that if he had still been alive, his granddaughter wouldn't be Queen. This is clearly beyond her comprehension.

'Oh well,' she says, 'I guess you couldn't have interviewed him. Not if he's dead.'

But I shouldn't be superior about all this. Why should she know these things?

Boston, 12 June 1984

The publishers' headquarters are near Boston so I finally meet Marcy Posner, who is handling the book tour. She and two other women are waiting in the foyer of the vast hotel (in which we are given a suite) to greet me. To my embarrassment, she hands me a huge bouquet. What the hell am I going to do with it? I dump it in our washbasin and we all go out to lunch. We sample, of course, clam chowder.

Last year, when we were in Paris, we one night had to share a table in a modest bistro with an American couple, called Robert and Maida Greenberg. As one does, we exchanged addresses, never dreaming that we would ever see each other again. Well, they live in Boston, so I telephone them and this evening they come round to see us. They are suitably impressed by the contrast between our two meetings: the first in that cheap and crowded restaurant in Paris, the second in this palatial suite in Boston.

Gallantly, I present a delighted Maida Greenberg with the bouquet.

Cleveland, 14 June 1984

Before coming to the States I'd worked out all sorts of clever things to say to interviewers – about the relevance of the monarchy today, the Queen's constitutional role, etc. I could have saved myself the trouble. The only questions I ever get asked are about 'Lady Di' or 'Princess Di'. Several people assume she is Margaret Thatcher's daughter. As I don't know all that much about her, I usually have to bluff my way through.

A prime example of this today. The studio is set out as a sort of cafe, with women sitting at little tables from which they lob questions at me. Viewers can also ring in with their questions. It is a live show. Before we start the chat-show host warns me never to say 'I don't know' or 'I'm not sure about that'. I must always have an answer ready. I manage pretty well until a call comes in from somewhere in Canada. A woman wants to know if it is true that 'Lady Di' sacked her butler for giving away her slimming secrets. Until that moment I'd never heard this story. I do some quick thinking and then announce, with all the conviction that I can muster, that I have researched the matter thoroughly, that I have discussed it with Her Royal Highness and that there is no truth in the rumour whatsoever. On to the next question.

[Some years later I told this story to an audience at one of those literary jamborees at Hay-on-Wye. Afterwards a man introduced himself as the Princess's butler and admitted that he had indeed given the story to a Canadian newspaper. But he hadn't been sacked.]

Los Angeles, 24 June 1984

Brian and I are walking up and down outside the building where I am to appear on the *Merv Griffin Show*. A young man darts up to offer us tickets for the show. I explain that I am on it; he clearly thinks that I am some sort of nutter. Once inside, I am told that my fellow guests are to be Shelley Winters, who is going to talk about her sex life; a French chanteuse who is going to sing a sexy song; and some woman who has just published a book called, I think, *The Happy Orgasm*. How the hell I am going to follow all this with a discussion on the British royal family, I just don't know.

My spirits are considerably cheered by the make-up man who manages to make me look about thirty-nine. His is the old story: he came to Hollywood decades ago in the hope of becoming a movie star and is now, I'm glad to say, a first-rate make-up artist. Shelley Winters, who is being attended by a bevy of make-up people, is wonderfully plump and expansive. She assures me that she 'just adores' the British royal family.

Two cups of coffee are a mistake and so, before going on,

I go to the 'rest room'. As I leave, I notice that a huge circle of wet has appeared on my trousers. Decide that it won't matter as I will be seen only from the waist up. I couldn't have been more wrong. I am led along endless corridors and am then ushered through a doorway of what turns out to be a vast, brilliantly lit stage with, in the dark beyond, an audience of hundreds of applauding people. All I can think about is the stain on my trousers. Keep my jacket as tightly closed as I can and walk across, in a daze, to where Merv Griffin is rising to greet me.

As an interviewer, Merv Griffin is reassuringly accomplished and avuncular. Can't really remember what I say except that, as usual, I say it too fast. He has been very well briefed and, unlike most chat-show hosts, isn't just working from the jacket blurb or the first chapter. He had once had dealings with the Duke and Duchess of Windsor: the Duke had landed himself, he says, with 'one bossy lady'.

To relieve the inevitable tension of doing the show, we decide to make our own way back. I ask if we can catch a bus back to the Beverly Hilton. This causes consternation. No one, apparently, ever takes buses here. Even the walk to the bus stop is regarded as suicidal. But I insist and, after much asking about among various workmen hammering in things, am told that we can get one from the bottom of the street. We stroll down unhindered ('You *were* on,' exclaims the man who had earlier tried to interest us in tickets for the show), wait at the shop in perfect safety, climb aboard a comfortable bus and are deposited right outside the hotel, all in considerably less time than it took the cab earlier in the day.

A message from Marcy Posner to say that she has managed to get me on to the *Nightwatch* show in Washington.

25 June 1984

Spend almost an hour in the cab which is taking me to some radio station for an interview. The woman interviewing me has not, of course, read my book, only the prologue, which is all about Queen Victoria's funeral. No matter how skilfully (and by now I am extremely skilled at this) I widen each question to cover other aspects of the book, back she goes to the prologue. The listeners must assume that I have written a 300-page study of Queen Victoria's funeral.

During the interminable drive back to the Beverly Hilton, when the cab stops at yet another traffic light, I see a small restaurant called Tregaron; opened, I imagined, by some Welsh ex-pat. Am immediately taken back to another Tregaron, which is no more than a shop and a couple of houses near Kirkwood in South Africa, where I was born. That Tregaron is where my Latvian-born father, in his early twenties in 1914, first lived on arriving in South Africa. How hot, dusty, desolate Tregaron must have struck my father, just out from the bustling port of Riga, I can't imagine. And of course, to my lasting regret, I never really asked. Five years after his arrival my father married my mother, a teacher by the name of Hannah Wilson, and built the house in Kirkwood in which they both died, within three months of each other, over fifty years later.

In the course of my great Napoleonic pilgrimage in 1956/ 7, I spent a few weeks with my parents in Kirkwood.

Although my mother travelled quite extensively, my father — having settled in Kirkwood — never left it again except to go to the nearest city, Port Elizabeth, about fifty miles away. There he sat, for year after year, decade after decade, going nowhere other than to Port Elizabeth, on either the Uitenhage or the Addo road. Well, I arrived home just before Christmas, very full of myself, having just made that 6,000-mile-long overland hitch-hiking journey. My father asked me which way I had come. I started to explain that I had travelled across Europe, through the Middle East and down Africa, but he cut me short.

'No, no,' he said, 'did you come through Uitenhage or through Addo?'

Washington, 27 June 1984

As I am waiting in the television studios for my appearance on *Nightwatch* someone comes up and says what I take to be 'Mr Aronson'. I follow him into a studio and am told to sit in a chair beside the interviewer. The interviewer, who is busy with his notes, hardly glances up. When he finally does speak to me, he addresses me as 'Senator'. I ask him why. 'Aren't you Senator Eagleton?' he asks. When I tell him who I am I am hustled out of the chair and Senator Eagleton, who has just resigned and is therefore hot news, is rushed into the room.

When my turn finally comes, I am deeply impressed by the interviewer. He has obviously done his homework and is, besides, wonderfully relaxed and articulate. He is one of those interviewers who brings out the best in me and we enjoy a highly successful session, full of laughs and anecdotes. When it's over, everyone crowds round to congratulate me. Perhaps it's just the American way, but I leave the studios feeling very gratified and not, as usual, vaguely dissatisfied.

Frome, 2 July 1984

While sorting through some files the other day I came across a press photograph of King George VI and Queen Elizabeth arriving to attend a banquet in the Cape Town city hall during their 1947 tour of South Africa. So I wrote to the Queen Mother to ask if she would kindly sign it for me. Back comes a letter from Alastair Aird to say that she would, but on condition that she approved of the photograph. If not, she will send me a signed copy of another, more recent one.

This reminds me of a story about an official in the Civil Service who, during the Second World War, sent to Buckingham Palace – on behalf of a unit of servicewomen in some remote station – a photograph of the Queen. Would Her Majesty be kind enough to sign the photograph so that it could be hung up in the canteen? The picture was a rare, pre-war one, showing the Queen in – possibly Guide's – uniform.

Back from the Palace came an extremely sharp refusal. Her Majesty was very surprised to receive such a request from an official in the Civil Service, apparently 'prepared to distribute the photograph at will'. After the abashed official had written back to explain the circumstances, he was forgiven. The servicewomen were rewarded with a large signed Cecil Beaton portrait of the Queen in a white sequined crinoline, diamond necklace and tiara.

The point is that the Queen Mother hated photographs of herself in uniform; in fact, as Queen, she never wore one. For one thing, she was the wrong shape; for another, it ran counter to her deliberate presentation of herself as a pretty-as-a-picture queen. She wanted the world always to see her as a romantic, feminine, flowery figure.

[Some years later, I asked her why, despite being commander-in-chief of several women's regiments, she was never seen in uniform during the war. 'There were too many of them,' she answered deftly. 'One would have been changing all day long.']

But clearly, she has no complaints about my photograph. Nor should she: she looks exactly as she likes to look – a child's version of a somewhat plump fairy queen. It arrives back today, duly signed – in ballpoint.

12 September 1984

I visit Mary Goldie [ex-secretary to the late Princess Alice, Countess of Athlone] who lives in retirement in a monumental block of flats at the Hammersmith end of the Kensington High Street. She seems almost pathetically pleased to see me. Within minutes I realize that she misses the old days tremendously. Then she was in the thick of things royal; now she has almost no contact with that world.

And whereas, when I first met her, Miss Goldie was rather reticent, now she is full of talk – a fund of information and anecdote.

She is especially interesting about the late ex-Queen Ena of Spain – born the daughter of Queen Victoria's youngest daughter Princess Beatrice, and consort of King Alfonso XIII. Far from being the austere, withdrawn figure of popular legend, living in doleful exile, ex-Queen Ena was a vivacious and amusing personality: 'a great giggler' as Mary Goldie puts it. She also had luxurious tastes. Whenever the ex-Queen visited Princess Alice at Kensington Palace, the Princess would be obliged to give over her own bedroom – the largest in the house – which Queen Ena would proceed to fill with her own possessions: fur rugs, sumptuous clothes, scents and cosmetics.

After tea, Mary Goldie offers me a drink. At five o'clock, it is too early for me but not wanting to seem prissy, I accept a small tot of whisky. She pours herself a somewhat larger one. As I leave, she is pouring herself another.

5 October 1984

June Botha, over from South Africa, brings an uncle and aunt to tea with us. They are an elderly couple, he rather doddery. His name is Harold Albert and about fifteen years ago he wrote a book called *Queen Victoria's Sister*. Luckily we have it and in next to no time he spots it on our shelves. Delighted, he signs it for us with the message 'by sheer coincidence'.

Tea over, he is clearly anxious to get away as, although June will be driving, he does not want to set off for home in the dark. When June suggests that we take her on a tour of Frome's antique and junk shops, he gets distinctly agitated and she has to give up the idea. They leave soon after five.

Although Harold Albert gives the impression that *Queen Victoria's Sister* is the only book he has ever written, we know that it is not. For he is 'Helen Cathcart', prolific writer of books about the present royal family. This is not even hinted at, let alone discussed, during today's visit. June, who knows the truth, has never breathed a word. As far as the general public is concerned, Helen Cathcart is a publicity-shy maiden lady, living in some inaccessible part of the Scottish Highlands, who can be contacted only through her agent – Harold Albert. In 'her' book about Sandringham House, which we also happen to have, Helen Cathcart slyly thanks Mr Harold A. Albert for 'editorial collaboration'.

Helen Cathcart has written dozens of the sort of bland, uncritical studies of the royal family which, in the past, have sold very well. 'She' has even produced a book called *The Queen and the Arts*, which is stretching hagiography a bit.

I wonder if Harold Albert suspects that we know his secret?

PART III

'I lived like a beatnik'

Princess Alice, Duchess of Gloucester, on her years in East Africa

Frome, 4 April 1985

FOR THE PAST year I've been busy on my new book, to be titled *Crowns in Conflict: The Triumph and Tragedy of European Monarchy 1910–1918*. One of the leading personalities in the study is the ineffable Queen Marie of Romania. On the last occasion that I saw the Queen Mother, we spoke about Queen Marie: about her beauty, vivacity and larger-than-life personality. 'She simply *filled* a room', was how the Queen Mother described her to me. I thought this to be a very graphic description, so have written to Alastair Aird to ask if I may quote the Queen Mother's phrase in my book.

Today's letter is a kind but firm refusal. Her Majesty cannot remember using that particular phrase. Instead, she suggests that I attribute to her another, extremely bland, description of the flamboyant Queen Marie: something along the lines of all heads turning whenever she entered a room.

I wonder why the Queen Mother doesn't want me to use her original phrase? It's hardly outrageous and Queen Marie has been dead for almost fifty years. Perhaps she feels it contains a hint of criticism and, canny professional that she is, the Queen Mother doesn't want to be caught slighting a fellow monarch. One of the Queen Mother's great strengths is that she has never expressed any controversial opinions in public. She has always kept her mouth for smiling.

9 April 1985

Brian gets an extraordinary, much-redirected letter today from a man claiming to be an Arab prince, a member of a Middle Eastern royal family. He has read a review of Brian's *The Mad, Bad Line*, which is full of the scandalous doings of Lord Alfred Douglas's family, and feels that Brian is just the man to write about similar dark goings-on among certain Middle Eastern monarchies. The letter comes from Mecca and is dated, according to the Islamic calendar, New Year's Day 1407. The writer is obliged, he assures Brian, to use a nom de plume. His suggestion is the usual one on these occasions: he will give Brian the information (a day's work); Brian will write the book (two years' work); and they will share the 'fortune' which the book is bound to make.

Brian gives him the customary answer. He is very busy. (He is writing his life of Cecil Rhodes.) As a full-time, professional writer he cannot undertake speculative work which may or may not be published. He suggests that his correspondent discuss the idea with a literary agent or publisher.

And that, I suspect, is the last we, or anyone, will ever hear of the 'Arab prince'.

27 April 1985

As my good deed for the day, I give a talk on 'Interviewing the Royals' to a senior citizens' group. Always my worst audience. They talk, they shuffle about, they fall asleep. At question time I'm asked no questions; instead, I'm regaled with anecdotes about how they once saw this or that member of the aristocracy, whom they lump together with the royals. But today one very old man does ask a question about a member of the royal family. 'Why haven't you mentioned Prince Edward?' he demands. I explain that I know very little about him and have never had anything to do with him. 'Is it true', he asks quaveringly, 'that he's a Mary-Anne?' Only because of my researches into the Victorian underworld do I know that the expression means 'gay'. I tell him that I have no idea.

12 May 1985

Am told an amusing story about the Queen and Margaret Thatcher. As the Prime Minister becomes progressively more regal, so does her attitude towards the Queen become slightly less obsequious and slightly more competitive. The other night she attended an official reception at Buckingham Palace and was disconcerted to find that both she and Her Majesty were wearing dresses of an identical shade of blue. On getting back to Downing Street, she sent a message to the Palace to say that, in future, she would like to be told what colour the Queen would be wearing, so that she could avoid it.

Back came an answer to the effect that the Prime Minister need have no worries on that score: Her Majesty never noticed what other women were wearing.

19 November 1985

Have written an extremely polite – not to say shamelessly sycophantic – letter to Princess Margaret to tell her that I was thinking of writing a book about her blighted romance with Group-Captain Peter Townsend in the 1950s. It would be, I assured her, a factual, sympathetic, responsible study, in no way sensationalized or trivialized. I asked for her opinion on this and whether, if she approved, she would be prepared to speak to me about it.

Today – a month later – brings a very dusty answer from her private secretary, Lord Napier. Her Royal Highness has no wish to see such a book written and would be unable to give me any assistance.

So that's that. Can't say I'm altogether surprised.

28 November 1985

There has recently been an article about me in a West Country newspaper, in which I am described as 'the Frome-based author'. Today I get a letter addressed to: 'Theo Aronson, Author, Frome-Based, Somerset'.

29 January 1986

I am commissioned by a magazine to write an article to mark the eighty-fifth birthday, in December, of Princess Alice, Duchess of Gloucester. I get a letter off to HRH to ask if she will give me an interview. Get an answer today from Sir

Simon Bland, the young Duke of Gloucester's private secretary, to say that Princess Alice will 'receive' me, at the end
of April, at Barnwell Manor, her country place in Northamptonshire. He suggests that I ring Miss Betty Chalmers,
HRH's secretary at Barnwell, to arrange a date.

3 February 1986

Ring Betty Chalmers who tells me that Princess Alice suggests
that I spend the night at Barnwell. We arrange for me to
arrive before lunch on Monday 28 April and leave after
breakfast the following day.

18 February 1986

My agent, George Greenfield (I switched from Gerald Pollinger some years ago), has been contacted by a television
company, Andrew Holmes Associates, who are planning to
make a documentary about the royal family from the death
of Queen Victoria until the marriage of Charles and Diana:
the very ground covered by my *Royal Family: Years of Transition*.

Go up to London today to meet Andrew Holmes in a
chaotic office off Oxford Street. He and the rest of his team
are all very young, in their twenties and thirties. Holmes
plans to make use of the current fad for converting old black-
and-white films into colour, by doing the same with old
newsreels. Although I don't approve of colouring in old films,
I don't suppose I object to a similar treatment for newsreels.
Am completely converted when he shows me an example of
the process: result is very subtle, not at all offensive.

Four of us — Andrew Holmes, his wife and a film-maker, if that's the term, called Nancy Platt — go out to lunch to discuss the project. I think they are surprised by my less than reverent attitude towards the royal family. They had obviously expected some uncritical, reactionary monarchist. We agree that I will write a script and advise on newsreels for the making of a ten-minute trailer which Holmes will use to raise American money for the project.

I'm rather looking forward to all this. It will make a welcome change from those lonely days, weeks and months at the desk.

19 March 1986

I've been up and down to London like a yo-yo during the past few weeks. I'm working most closely with the highly professional Nancy Platt: viewing old newsreels, deciding what to use, revising my script. I'm struck by how little they know about the subject. The most hackneyed royal phrases and anecdotes, which I hesitate to use, come as completely fresh to them. At one stage I realize that Nancy thinks that the young Queen Elizabeth — consort of King George VI — is the young Queen Elizabeth II. 'Wasn't she *fat* in those days!' she exclaims. To her, the 1950s are as remote as the 1930s.

On the other hand, I realize that they find my approach and language too formal. Quite rightly, they keep reminding me that the series has to make sense in Des Moines, Iowa.

They are astonished that I have no video recorder, so arrange for me to hire one for a month. From then on Brian and I watch, not only films supplied by them with titles like *The Glittering Crowns* and *Princess* but lots of movies hired from our local video shop.

Most of these people I'm working with tend to be anti-monarchist. They see the monarchy as an outdated, worthless, extravagant institution. They cannot understand why the Queen doesn't speak out on national issues; although I'm sure they'd be the first to complain if she said something of which they didn't approve. And I'm amused at the way in which these progressive, open-minded people are quick to point out that Sarah Ferguson, whose engagement to Prince Andrew has just been announced, has what they call a 'track record' — that she lived with another man before her engagement.

22 March 1986

Spend the night in Nancy Platt's little house in London because we must be up at first light for a day's filming. We are going to shoot the linking bits between the newsreels. These are to be spoken by an American actor called Ed Bishop. He turns out to be a handsome, unflurried professional, who does it all beautifully. He even remembers to congratulate me on my script. We career from St Paul's Cathedral to Buckingham Palace to Windsor Castle and back to Westminster Abbey.

I, who had never heard of Ed Bishop, am astonished by the number of people who obviously have: heads keep turning as we pass. While we are filming outside Westminster Abbey, a car screeches to a halt and, double yellow lines notwithstanding, a young man leaps out and dashes up to Ed Bishop for his autograph.

3 April 1986

Have written to Betty Chalmers at Barnwell Manor to ask if I need bring a dinner jacket or just a dark suit. A dark suit, she writes to tell me, is 'exactly the correct thing to wear' and will I please bring some sunshine with me.

22 April 1986

We watch the first completed version of the royal family trailer. It's really very good. Let's hope that Andrew Holmes can raise the necessary money to make the series. [He never did, and the project, like so many television projects, died a death. Money down the drain but at least I was paid a handsome fee, plus expenses.]

25 April 1986

I have flu and have been feeling absolutely dreadful for the last few days. Have even taken to my bed, which is something I seldom do. Whenever I am ill, the first thing to go is my appetite; I simply cannot eat a mouthful. And although I am feeling slightly better today, I still cannot eat. Most worrying of all is the fact that I have to drive up to Barnwell Manor in Northamptonshire on Monday and somehow force myself to eat lunch, dinner and breakfast. Am dreading it.

Am saved by a telephone call from Betty Chalmers this

morning. The Duchess of Windsor died yesterday and Princess Alice will have to attend the funeral at Windsor next week. So would I mind 'dreadfully' if my visit was postponed for a couple of weeks? Not only would I not mind dreadfully, I would not mind at all. In fact, I instantly feel better.

How strange that I should be personally involved, even at one stage removed, with the funeral of the Duchess of Windsor. I remember the announcement of King Edward VIII's abdication very clearly. If it came as a surprise to most people in Britain, it certain came as one in Kirkwood. I had just turned seven at the time. We had a family friend staying with us – an elegant, unmarried school inspectress who was not unlike a fair-haired version of Wallis Simpson – and I can still hear my mother saying, jokingly, 'You could have married him, Mattie.'

And now here I am, fifty years later, having to postpone a visit to one of the few remaining players in the abdication drama, because of Wallis Simpson's funeral.

Port Erin, 5 May 1986

My sister Peggy's birthday. Brian and I are on the Isle of Man where I give my talk on 'Writing Royal Biography' to the local branch of the Society of Authors. The event has been organized by the writer Vivien Allen who lives on the island. The other speaker is P. D. James and last night's closing banquet was addressed by Magnus Magnusson. Am sure that the majority of those attending would prefer to be given tips on how to write successfully for Mills and Boon.

Am cornered by a journalist named Monica O'Hara who is a graphologist – an analyser of handwriting. She has analysed the Duke of Windsor's handwriting – 'full of mental anguish and friction' – and has decided that he was, among other things, impotent. She quizzes me on this and on her other conclusions, to which I give non-committal replies.

[All this subsequently appears in an article about me in the *Liverpool Echo* under the headline 'The "royal" seal of approval.']

Barnwell Manor, 15 May 1986

I set off in the Mini at nine this morning, imagining that this will give me plenty of time to reach Barnwell by lunchtime. But I go wrong in the confusion of roads beyond Northampton and arrive just before one. The first view of Barnwell is of an ancient, crumbling castle standing in the grounds of the estate; the second is of the house itself – a sprawling, honey-coloured manor house in a mixture of styles. Inside, the atmosphere is that of a grand English country house: comfortable, slightly shabby, full of books, flowers and pictures.

My overnight bag is taken by a young manservant – obviously a local farm boy doing his best to act the royal butler – and I am led up to my room. Huge, with a wonderfully old-fashioned bathroom and a splendid view. Betty Chalmers, plump and friendly, dashes up to tell me that I must insist on the Princess going for her nap after lunch and not keep her talking for more than half an hour or so.

Princess Alice is waiting for me in the drawing room. 'You

find a very depressed old lady,' she says jokingly, indicating the rain which is bucketing down. But she seems neither depressed nor as old as her years. During lunch we discuss what are obviously two favourite household topics: the weather and the traffic. She and Betty Chalmers love the idea of my having lost my way. I regale them with funny stories about the other Princess Alice, the late Countess of Athlone.

After lunch and again after her nap, Princess Alice answers my questions. When I ask if marrying into the royal family (in 1935, at the age of thirty-four) had dramatically changed her life, she answers wryly, 'No, I was very used to that sort of life.' Indeed, as the daughter of the seventh Duke of Buccleuch, she had grown up in no fewer than five palatial homes. So when, as a girl, she was once told by a fortune-teller that she would marry someone of 'a higher station' she could hardly believe it. 'Since I was a duke's daughter,' she says, 'this seemed unlikely to me.'

We talk about her public duties which, in her eighties, she still undertakes. 'It would just never occur to her', the Duke of Gloucester's private secretary once said to me, 'to turn anything down.' Shy, stiff and self-effacing, she forces herself to play her royal role. 'Nowadays everyone in the royal family works much harder than we used to when I was young,' she explains. 'The local lord of the manor took care of many of the things we have to attend to now.' She hates travelling to engagements by helicopter. 'You get out, there's this frightful noise, and, half-deaf, you are expected to make polite conversation over it.'

Now and then her wry sense of humour comes out. I comment on an exotic flowering plant in the corner and wonder how it can possibly survive indoors. 'It was brought in this morning, for your benefit,' she says. 'It goes back into the greenhouse tomorrow.'

When the rain stops we walk in the garden. Here she is at her happiest. To me the garden — with its great expanses of lawn, clipped hedges, flower borders and gnarled old trees — looks magnificent. 'It's not like it was in the old days when we had half a dozen gardeners,' she sighs. 'Nowadays I seem to spend my time fighting a war against weeds.' In a large shed I notice a pile of unused garden benches, all with brass plaques: presented, I imagine, by organizations or regiments who imagined that they had found the perfect gift.

The Princess tells me that I needn't change for dinner (I am in a tweed jacket) but as I've brought my dark suit — a newish one — I may as well make use of it. She wears a kaftan. We eat at a small table set in front of the fire in the drawing room: soup, chops, apple crumble.

We talk about East Africa. Once, on an extensive jaunt around East Africa — Zanzibar, Mombasa, Dar es Salaam — I pitched up, penniless, in Nairobi. So I worked in the J. Walter Thompson Nairobi office for a month, before setting off again. As an unmarried young woman, the Princess spent seven years, off and on, in East Africa living — as she somewhat fancifully puts it — like 'a beatnik'. This entailed moving, as I understand it, between government houses and country estates. Not appreciating that thirty years separated our respective East African visits, she asks if I knew this or that person, all governors, district commissioners, or estate owners — exactly the sort of people I would never have met.

Her East African photograph albums, which she leaves for

me to look at while she is having her nap, are full of pictures of a wildly attractive young man. I don't ask who he is. He is certainly a far cry from the stolid prince whom she eventually married.

The Princess has the prejudices of her class and generation. Most of the new African states are 'communist'. On the other hand, all the Africans now care about is money. 'They expect to be paid if you photograph them,' she grumbles. 'In the old days, you just gave them a safety-pin and they were very grateful.'

After dinner we watch the news on television and see the Prince and Princess of Wales in Japan, attending a sumo wrestling match. 'Poor things,' she comments. She takes me up to my room and explains that, once in it, I am not to leave it. 'The minute you set foot on the threshold', she warns, 'all the alarms go off and the police come dashing in.' I feel, for no good reason, trapped. But why should I need to leave the room, when I have my own bathroom?

Frome, 16 May 1986

At Barnwell, I eat breakfast alone: cereal and a poached egg. Betty Chalmers bounces in with a detailed map and we plan my route home. The Princess, in corduroy trousers, comes down to see me off. I sign the visitors' book and wait for my Mini, which has been washed and polished, to be driven up. As I drive away I see the Princess, with the much less enthusiastic looking Betty Chalmers in tow, setting out into the garden for yet another assault on the encroaching ground elder.

I leave Barnwell with the impression that for all her nervous mannerisms, Princess Alice is a woman of great strength of character: self-disciplined, resilient, conscientious. And she couldn't have been nicer to me.

27 May 1986

Spend the day in London doing bits of publicity for *Crowns in Conflict* including a radio interview with, of all unlikely people, Chris Tarrant. I find that one of the difficulties in talking about *Crowns in Conflict*, or any book, is that it was completed over a year ago and that I am already deep into the next one. My latest subject was suggested by John Murray himself: a study of the three so-called official mistresses of King Edward VII – Lillie Langtry, Daisy Warwick and Alice Keppel. Fascinating stuff.

Go to Clarence House with a gift copy of *Crowns in Conflict* for the Queen Mother. On arriving, I find that yesterday's bad weather has delayed her flight back from Scotland. I hand the book over to Alastair Aird. Two minor points of interest. I chat to one of the Queen Mother's ladies-in-waiting, Lady Fermoy, a faded beauty who is the grandmother of the Princess of Wales and who is rumoured to have engineered the marriage of her granddaughter to Prince Charles. And I see a huge dress box (if that is what it's called) from Hartnell containing, I daresay, yet another of the Queen Mother's all-but-identical summer outfits. 'Not *another* new dress, Mummy!' the Queen is said to complain at her mother's lavish spending on clothes. Not that the Queen Mother takes the slightest notice.

17 August 1986

A letter from Princess Alice who has been sent a proof of my article on her. I had explained that the silly title, 'Born a Lady', had nothing to do with me. The letter, in her own, scrawling hand, corrects a few minor errors. There is some doubt, she writes, that the whole royal family will be gathering at Windsor Castle, as customary, for Christmas. I suspect that the Queen finds this annual jamboree – including the likes of Princess Michael of Kent – too much and that, from now on, only the inner core of the family will get together – at Sandringham.

Leningrad, 18 September 1986

We are spending two weeks in Russia, on a long-promised holiday. This morning we go to Pushkin, which used to be called Tsarskoe Selo, where Nicholas II and his family lived. The restoration of these Russian imperial palaces is incredible. I believe that Lenin said that whatever one thought of the old imperial regime, these palaces were all part of Russia's national heritage and had to be maintained.

The Catherine Palace, bombed to bits by the Germans during the Second World War, is now like new, all a-glitter with gold leaf. The Alexander Palace, where Nicholas and Alexandra lived, is, says our guide meaningfully, 'strictly forbidden'. I ask her where in the grounds Rasputin is buried. She turns ashen and takes me aside. How do I know that Rasputin is buried there? I say that I have read about it in biographies of Rasputin and of the imperial family and in histories of the Russian revolution. She is astonished. 'It is all a big secret,' she whispers. She also assures us that the fate of Nicholas and Alexandra and their family remains a mystery. 'They took the money and the jewels and went away in a train,' she says. 'Nobody knows where they went.' Any other theories are simply 'legends believed in the West'.

I presume she really believes all this.

Later, we go to St Peter's and St Paul's Cathedral to see the tombs of the tsars. I wonder if glasnost will ever reach the stage where the authorities will admit the truth about the murder of the imperial family at Ekaterinburg and bring back the remains of Tsar Nicholas II for burial here?

19 September 1986

This afternoon Brian and I escape from the group and brave the metro. We wander around this stage-set of a city and stroll down Nevsky Prospect looking for the Yusupov Palace, where Rasputin was murdered. No luck. Saying the name 'Yusupov' to assorted ladies in headscarves brings blank stares.

Walking back to the hotel we stray off a zebra crossing just before it meets the pavement. We are bellowed at by a policeman who fines us three roubles (about three pounds) on the spot. Not a car, of course, in sight.

St Helier, 1 October 1986

We are on Jersey where I am researching Lillie Langtry for my book on Edward VII's mistresses. Have been given the name of an old man who is said to be the authority on Lillie Langtry and her liaison with the then Prince of Wales. I meet him and within a few minutes realize that he knows nothing: nothing other than the information he has gleaned from reading Lillie Langtry's own ultra discreet and highly unreliable book of memoirs. He has simply copied out sentences from her book (a copy of which I have anyway owned for years) which he proceeds to read out to me.

I have more luck with a man called Monins who has, in his large house on the north coast, an extraordinarily comprehensive collection of material relating to the island, among which is a great deal of stuff on Lillie Langtry. Every modern aid to research, in the way of computers, photostat machines, etc., is available and at my disposal, so we spend a profitable day there.

[Some time later the so-called authority on Lillie writes, offering to read my finished typescript 'for mistakes'.]

Frome, 15 October 1986

I get a letter from Joan Lascelles. She wants to know if Brian and I will be in 'the beautiful Cape' [Cape Town, South Africa] this winter. She has the mistaken idea that we spend the summers in Frome, the winters in Kommetjie. If only. For her, alas, the glory days — when she and Princess Alice were lavishly entertained and accommodated by Cape Town's leading hostesses — are over. Once Princess Alice died, doors tended to close for poor Joan Lascelles. She still goes out every winter for several months but now she stays in a modest boarding house.

[Joan Lascelles died in South Africa the following year. During her last illness, she happened to be in the hospital bed next to one occupied by the sister of our Kommetjie friend Ann Seeliger. Ann was a great talker and in no time discovered that Joan not only knew Kommetjie but knew Brian and me. Joan Lascelles was buried in Cape Town. And although, on our next visit out there, the British Consulate-General promised to let me know where she was buried, they never did.]

Cambridge, 27 January 1987

We are spending a few days in Cambridge where I am looking at the seven-volume diaries of Wilfrid Scawen Blunt in the Fitzwilliam Museum for *The King in Love: Edward VII's Mistresses*. Blunt was friendly with the celebrated Victorian courtesan, Catherine Walters, usually known as 'Skittles'. From her he garnered all sorts of information about the royal family: about Queen Victoria's relationship with John Brown, Edward VII's 'impotence' (he had been one of Skittles's many lovers) and about the King's arranging for the return of his many letters to her when it seemed as though she might be dying.

He also tells a bizarre story about Queen Victoria's daughter, the 'artistic' Princess Louise, being in love with the sculptor, Edgar Boehm, and being discovered in a 'compromising position' with Boehm by the Queen. A 'violent scene' followed during which Louise threatened to make a public scandal of the Queen's relationship with Brown.

Elizabeth Longford, who has written the biography of Wilfrid Scawen Blunt, has warned me that much of what he says has to be treated with caution. I exercise considerable caution but, nevertheless, manage to come away with a great deal of fascinating, and verifable, information. (Brian's fingers are almost numb from copying-out.)

London, 28 January 1987

Our agent, George Greenfield, is retiring, and Andrew Lownie, who has been working with him, is anxious for Brian and me to join the agency which he is setting up. We meet him for the first time this evening, when he gives us dinner at the Oxford and Cambridge Club. He is younger than we had imagined; good-looking, gentlemanly and enthusiastic. He wears a hat, which is unusual these days. (Whatever happened to my hats?) We agree to join his agency.

Frome, 4 March 1987

A journalist called Andrew Morton telephones me. He is writing a book about the various royals living in Kensington Palace. I give him what help I can. (The Palace was called the 'Aunt Heap' a few generations ago because so many royal widows lived there: I daresay it will be called that again in the not-too-distant future.) What I don't tell Andrew

Morton is that his is exactly the sort of book that doesn't sell. He had better not give up the day job.

25 March 1987

We go to Trowbridge to see about Brian's typewriter. On the way back to the car, we find the pavement blocked by a little crowd of people. We are told that 'royalty' is expected. A few seconds later a Daimler draws up, a schoolmistress instructs a group of schoolchildren to start cheering and wave their little paper flags, and out steps Princess Alice, Duchess of Gloucester. She looks very elegant, quite different from the last time I saw her in trousers and headscarf. She is apparently due to inaugurate − if that's the word − a new hall.

I wonder if anyone in the crowd knows who she is? I doubt it. Am sure that the schoolchildren were hoping for Diana.

5 April 1987

A double coincidence day.

I dash into a little shelter in the Market Yard to escape a sudden squall of rain. There is a woman already sheltering in there and we chat. Or rather, in my fashion, I ask her questions. She is visiting Frome and once lived on the Copper Belt in Northern Rhodesia, now Zambia, My sister and brother-in-law, Jean and Peter Pitchford, once lived there and, yes, she knew them.

She asks me what work I do in Frome. I tell her that I am

a writer. What sort of books do I write? I hate this, as my
reply is usually met by a polite 'How interesting. It must take
a lot of research.' Or worse: 'I suppose they are used in
schools.' But this time she seems genuinely interested. I
explain that I have written books about various European
royal dynasties and personalities. 'You didn't write *Grandmama
of Europe*, did you?'

I did indeed.

16 May 1987

I get sent a book from the 'Continental Historical Society' of
San Francisco. It sets out to prove that the author of *Alice in
Wonderland* and *Through the Looking Glass* was not Lewis Carroll
(Charles Dodgson) but Queen Victoria. 'Computer studies'
apparently, have supplied this proof; the 'secret code' which
was 'finally cracked' after 'ten years of effort', reveals that the
Alice books are really the story of Queen Victoria's 'gruesome
childhood'.

21 May 1987

I have been asked by a magazine to do a piece on the young
Duchess of Gloucester. [She was born Birgitte van Deurs and,
before her marriage to Prince Richard of Gloucester, had
been a secretary at the Danish Embassy in London.] Today
brings a letter from the Duke's secretary, Sir Simon Bland, to
say that the Duchess never gives interviews; not even, he adds
graciously, 'to so distinguished a writer as yourself'.

London, 29 May 1987

I am a speaker at the Royal Stuart Society's annual 'Restoration Day Dinner' at Brown's Hotel. This is, I presume, on the strength of my having written, some years ago, a book entitled *Kings over the Water: The Saga of the Stuart Pretenders*.

We get into our dinner jackets (we are staying with Keith Killby) and being — as always — early, decide to have a glass of wine in the bar at Brown's. These cost us £3.50 each. Other speakers are the Duke of St Albans and the Earl of Lauderdale, who turn out to be exactly what one would expect at a gathering like this. (The punchline of one of the speakers' jokes is that the man turned out to be 'a socialist', at which everyone falls about.)

An odd collection of people: all believers, I presume, in the doctrine of the Divine Right of Kings, although I must admit that most of those I speak to don't have the slightest idea of what it is all about — other than a good evening out. The food is standard banquet catering — consommé, chicken, and strawberry mousse — and, to much applause, a piper marches around the table. All in all, a strange evening.

We are off to Paris tomorrow.

Frome, 14 June 1987

Hugo Vickers has asked Brian and me to take part in a book fair being held in the gardens of a country house near Oxford. We fill the boot with boxes of our books (knowing that we will be bringing most of them back) and set off.

Among the other stallholders are Sarah Bradford, H. R. F. Keating, Miss Read and Christopher Warwick; and the fair is opened (he is so late that it should read 'closed') by John Mortimer.

Am very interested to meet Roddy Llewellyn, whose affair with Princess Margaret, seventeen years his senior, was one of the great royal scandals of the 1970s. He is very attractive, very sexy, and his gardening books are selling like mad.

7 November 1987

A little dinner party to mark the publication of Brian's *Cecil Rhodes: Flawed Colossus*. Werner [Seehof] and Andrew [Wall] bring, as well as a bottle of champagne, a girl called Hazel [Wood] who works on the books page of the *Sunday Telegraph*. Brian is annoyed by Auberon Waugh's review in the *Independent* ('Just to be reviewed by Auberon Waugh is something,' says Hazel) but greatly cheered by William Boyd's glowing review in the *Spectator*.

Port Alfred, 11 March 1988

We are spending six weeks in South Africa and today an ageing reporter arrives to interview me. He has obviously come with a fixed idea of what I will be like: other worldly, living in the past, unconcerned with everyday affairs. Nothing I say can shake his mental picture of me. He also sees me as a passionate monarchist, but of the, by now, old-fashioned South African variety: in which all English-speakers were monarchists and Afrikaners republicans. His language is equally dated. [In his subsequent piece – by which time he has obviously heard me give one of my talks – I emerge as 'although being of a retiring disposition, and scholarly tastes, Aronson proves to have an unsuspected flair for public speaking, thinking on his feet, facing a quick ball, and cracking it away to the verbal boundary.'] Bizarre.

Cape Town, 23 March 1988

We are again staying with Joy Collier and living in a blur of reunions, parties, press and radio interviews and book signings – Brian for his *Cecil Rhodes: Flawed Colossus* and me for *The King in Love* – advance copies of which have been sent out here. John Murray telephones from London today to say that the American publishers, Harper and Row, have offered a big advance for my book. To celebrate, we take Joy to the sort of place we haven't been to for years: a restaurant with a dance floor. As I love dancing, we have a jolly evening.

Johannesburg, 7 April 1988

We are staying here with Percy Tucker and Graham Dickason. Having driven up, in a hired car, from Port Alfred, we had been due to spend last night at a hotel called Riverside Lodge on the Lesotho border. Years ago, when my sister Peggy lived in what was then Basutoland, Riverside Lodge was a superbly run place; now it is like something out of Tennessee Williams, entirely gone to seed. So, instead of staying there, we drove on. But this evening John Murray telephones to say that (on my brother-in-law Peter Pitchford's advice) he had rung me at the Riverside Lodge to find out if I could appear on the *Pebble Mill at One* show as soon as I arrive back in Britain. As he could not get hold of me there, he had had to pass up the opportunity. But he feels sure that they will be able to fit me in at a later date. Maddening.

Frome, 13 April 1988

We take the train from Bristol to Birmingham for my appearance on *Pebble Mill*. Other guests are the actor Brian Murphy, the writer Tim Severin and the TV chef Glyn Christian. Am interviewed by Pamela Armstrong. Immediately after the interview I get a telephone call from a woman who tells me that she has a 'very old, very rare royal book' which had once belonged to her grandmother; she would like to know what it is worth. It turns out to be a copy of *Queen Alexandra's Christmas Gift Book*, which was published in 1908 and 'sold for charity', copies of which are to be found in almost every second-hand bookshop in the land. She assures me that it has Queen Alexandra's 'own photographs' in it, and clearly doesn't believe me when I tell her that they are reproductions. It's always difficult to disillusion these people; all I can do is to suggest that she consults a bookseller.

14 April 1988

The London *Evening Standard* telephones this morning to ask me for a story to use in 'Londoner's Diary' about *The King in Love*. They will call back. They don't, but this afternoon

Murray's publicity girl rings to say that a piece has gone in, headed 'Royal qualms over birthday book'. It claims that I have written a 'salacious' book about the Queen's great-grandfather and that a 'courtier' has complained that the book has been especially published to 'cash in' on the Queen's birthday celebrations on 21 April. The book will, says the *Evening Standard*, 'ruin her day'.

All invention, of course. The Queen is in Australia at present. But as I am rather worried about this, I ring John Murray. He is not the slightest bit worried. On the contrary, he expects the orders to come rolling in from the booksellers.

Guernsey, 18 April 1988

I am at the Government House Hotel on Guernsey where I give a talk on 'Writing Royal Biography' to an obviously well-heeled audience at a luncheon. Sign lots of books. Meet three especially interesting people. One is Tony Carey, who organized the visit, and who turns out to be a descendant of the infamous Captain Carey, whose panicky behaviour led to the death of the Prince Imperial in the Zulu War of 1879. Another is Giles St Aubyn, a fellow writer on royal subjects who now lives on the island and whose family owns another island – St Michael's Mount, off Cornwall. The third is Joan Bagley, whose late husband, Desmond Bagley, was a highly successful adventure-story writer. (Like all such writers, he looked as though he wouldn't harm a fly.)

Frome, 9 May 1988

The London-based representative of an American magazine has invited me to lunch at the Ritz. He is apparently 'greatly impressed' by *The King in Love* and is anxious to interview me. He is very handsome, very smooth, full of blandishments. Within seconds I can tell that he hasn't actually read my 'brilliant' book; one always knows. But his chief preoccupation is with this morning's great scandal: that Major Ronald Ferguson, father of 'Fergie' – the Duchess of York – has been discovered visiting a massage parlour. He clearly thinks that this will deal the monarchy a mortal blow. 'How much more can the monarchy *take*?' he exclaims. My explanation that Major Ferguson is not a member of the royal family and that he has nothing whatsoever to do with the institution of monarchy, cuts no ice. 'I can't see how they will recover from this one,' he insists.

The reason why he wants to see me gradually becomes apparent. He is planning an article on the breakdown of the Wales's marriage and wants some 'inside' information. He obviously doesn't believe me when I say that I know very little about it. Surely, he insists, the subject must have come up during my 'meetings up with' the Queen Mother, Princess Margaret and other family members. When it becomes clear that I'm going to be of no use to him whatsoever, he loses interest and the meal ends with me having to push the conversation along. As we part, he says that he will let me know if the magazine wants an article on me and my 'brilliant' book.

At least I got a damn good lunch out of the whole abortive exercise.

29 May 1988

The King in Love has been on the bestseller lists for five weeks now. It has brought a flood, not only of reviews and correspondence but of letters and telephone calls from people claiming to be the illegitimate descendants of Edward VII. In spite of reading my book (or perhaps they haven't) in which I make clear that Edward's three-year-long liaison with Lillie Langtry was over by 1880, many of these correspondents claim descent from some child born to King Edward VII and Lillie in the early 1900s, when she was well past childbearing age.

Often the evidence is no stronger than the fact that someone's grandfather 'looked' like Edward VII – that, in short, he had a beard and a moustache and a paunch – hardly unusual in Victorian and Edwardian men. And the country is obviously chock-a-block with grand old ladies whose 'regal bearing', 'beautiful manners' and a striking resemblance to – not the King's own daughters but – Queen Mary, prove that they are the illegitimate daughters of King Edward VII.

One persistent woman caller has asked me to send her the guest lists of all the house parties ever held at Sandringham during the fifty years of Edward VII's association with the house. If her grandmother is on one of those lists, she assures me, then her own royal descent will be proved beyond question. Why? Even he didn't sleep with *every* woman guest, much less get every woman guest pregnant. Why I should put myself to the trouble and expense of getting hold of such lists – even if I could – obviously doesn't occur to my caller.

Others have stories about secret 'love nests' or underground passages which the King would use when entertaining Lillie Langtry (it is always her, never the other mistresses) despite the fact that by the time he became King, the affair had been over for a couple of decades.

There are, though, two genuine and very interesting illegitimate links between King Edward VII and the future British monarch, Prince Charles. Lillie Langtry had an illegitimate daughter by Prince Louis of Battenberg. Prince Louis later married one of Queen Victoria's granddaughters; and one of their grandsons was Prince Philip, Duke of Edinburgh, the father of Prince Charles. By this route are the descendants of Lillie Langtry, mistress of the future King Edward VII, related to the future King Charles III.

The other link concerns Edward VII's last and most important mistress, Alice (Mrs George) Keppel. It is more than likely that Alice's second daughter, Sonia, was fathered by the King, as she was born after their liaison had started. In time, Sonia Keppel married Ronald Cubitt: their granddaughter is Camilla Parker Bowles. At one stage Prince Charles had hoped to marry Camilla Shand, as she then was. The rumours that the two of them have re-established a close personal relationship seem to be well-founded.

17 June 1988

Between us, John Murray and I have decided that my next book will be a double biography of Napoleon and Josephine.

So I am returning, in a way, to my first love. Brian is also writing for Murray's: he is busy on *Those Bloody Women*, about three contrasting 'heroines' in the Boer War.

27 June 1988

I get up early to be ready for a telephone call from Sydney, Australia: I am to be interviewed, live, about *The King in Love*. As I still have half an hour in hand, I put on the kettle to make a cup of tea. The phone rings, earlier than expected, and a man asks if I am ready to do my interview immediately, reminding me that it is live. I agree, and settle down to do my bit.

Several minutes into the interview, I am distracted, first by a strange hissing noise and then by the room filling up with steam: I have left the kettle on. I can think of nothing other than the kettle boiling dry. In the end, there is nothing for it but to put down the phone and dash into the kitchen to switch off the kettle.

When the interview is over, the interviewer complains that he lost sound for a few seconds. 'It's the British telephone system,' I tell him. 'Dreadful. It happens all the time.'

2 August 1988

My talks to various women's groups bring home to me the odd attitude of many of them towards the royal family. The older generation, particularly, tends to regard the royals, not as ordinary people in an extraordinary position, but as almost superhuman. They will say things like 'she was so close to me I could have touched her' or 'he looked straight into my eyes'. One woman wonders if the Queen's hands have actually touched the invitation to a Buckingham Palace garden party received by her daughter. This same invitation is now framed. Even someone like the rollicking Duchess of York is instantly imbued with the royal mystique and becomes a person apart.

It's not so difficult to understand why Russian peasants working in the fields used to fall to their knees as the Tsar's train thundered by.

Paris, 18 September 1988

In France to refresh my memory of various Napoleonic sites for *Napoleon and Josephine*. Today we visit Malmaison. Brian and I first came here in August 1957, a couple of months after we met. It's the one place where one comes closest to understanding the relationship between Napoleon and Josephine. The house has been much restored since we last saw it; more than ever, it seems to capture something of the bittersweet quality of their life together.

Afterwards we walk to the nearby town of Rueil, where Josephine is buried. I have never been here before. Nor, it seems, have many others. Her tomb turns out to be extraordinarily difficult to find. Enquiries as to its whereabouts are met, not only by the people in the street but from the gendarmerie, with a shrug. It turns out to be in an unremarkable little church in a square in the heart of the town, although there is nothing outside to indicate this.

Yet, in her day, as Napoleon's Empress, Josephine was probably the most celebrated woman in the world: the Jackie

Onassis or Diana, Princess of Wales, of her time. While Napoleon's tomb is one of the great sights of Paris, hers is all but forgotten.

Frome, 7 February 1989

A letter today from a reader in Kent addressed simply to 'Theo Aronson, Author, Frome'. He is interested in a dog which appears in one of the photographs in *The King in Love*. The dog, he tells me, is 'a special breed' and he wants to know how he can get a copy of the photograph. All news to me. I look at the illustration – twenty members of a Victorian house party lined up for the camera – and can only just make out an indeterminate-looking black dog. Doesn't look a special breed to me. Write back with what information I can. He didn't even say that he had enjoyed reading the book.

24 February 1989

My niece, Jess Pitchford, is over here on an extended visit from South Africa, doing all sorts of odd jobs – sandwich-making, cooking, housesitting – to keep going. At present she is looking after an ancient brigadier and his wife and among their books she discovers a copy of my *Princess Alice: Countess of Athlone*. She tells the brigadier that it was written by her uncle. He obviously doesn't believe her. In his eyes she is simply a colonial-born home help who couldn't possibly be related to someone capable of writing a book about a member of the royal family.

Jersey, 30 May 1989

A chaotic day. The woman handling the publicity for the Corgi paperback of *The King in Love* has always insisted on sending everything to me – even the most unimportant letter – by special delivery. This means that instead of things arriving by the morning post, they have to be delivered, by van, from Bristol. Invariably I am out when the van arrives, and Brian, whose study is on the top floor, cannot hear the bell. So they leave me a card and ask me to ring the Bristol office. I ring and they arrange to make a delivery the following day. They can never give me an exact – not even an approximate – time, which means that I must wait in.

This morning I am due to fly to Jersey for a television interview for the book. The publishers are meant to be sending me some photographs of Lillie Langtry to be featured in the interview. As usual they were sent by special delivery and, as usual, we were not in when they called yesterday. This morning, with Brian having gone to the bank, I wait for the van. We must leave for Bristol airport by ten. I wait and wait. Finally, bursting to pee, I dash upstairs. I'm hardly there before the bell rings. I dash down again. The wretched card is on the mat and as I wrench open the door, I see the van driving away. So no pictures.

The flight to Jersey is delayed. Having finally arrived, there is no time to go to the hotel so we take a cab directly to the television studios. I arrive on the dot. No one knows anything about me. And the man who might have known is away. I sit for an hour. Finally, a girl arrives to do the interview. She also knows nothing about me nor, for that matter, about Lillie Langtry. I fill her in as best I can. We go, not into a studio but into the car park. There, in a howling wind, I do my stuff. Glad to hear that it will not be transmitted until next Thursday, by which time we will be safely back in Frome.

Ely, 14 August 1989

We are driving round Norfolk: huge, wonderful skies that remind me of South Africa. Today we visit Sandringham House. Even more hideous than I had expected. When one thinks of all the houses that could have served as a royal residence for the future King Edward VII, the choice of this red-brick pile is incomprehensible. It looks like the home of some nouveau-riche industrialist. (Can't pretend to be the first to say that.) The same thing, of course, is true of the house which Prince Andrew has just had built.

Vienna, 10 September 1989

Brian and I are on holiday, visiting Vienna and Budapest. For no apparent reason, we are being accommodated in an extremely grand hotel, right opposite Schönbrunn Palace, originally built to house the overflow of the Emperor Franz Josef's guests. It is not the hotel we chose — or paid for. Still, we're certainly not complaining. Stella [Collie and Stella Hill, our friends who happen to be on the same tour] feels sure that it is because the tour operators 'know who you are'. Flattering but entirely false.

It's over thirty years since I was last in Vienna. For all the changes, it remains an unmistakably imperial city. They still sell postcards of Franz Josef and Elisabeth as though they were alive.

Today we went out to Mayerling, scene of the famous suicide pact of Crown Prince Rudolph and Mary Vetsera in 1889 – almost exactly a hundred years ago. Very disappointing. A memorial chapel has been built on the site of the incident, which means that all the atmosphere of this one-time hunting lodge has been obliterated. One would imagine, from the hushed and holy air, that poor, feckless, frustrated Rudolph had been some sort of saint.

Tomorrow we sail down the Danube to Budapest.

Frome, 23 February 1990

A letter from John Murray today asking me to sign a slip of paper 'For Sally' which they will paste into a copy of *The King in Love* for a reader in Jersey. So at least one copy has been sold as a result of my windswept television appearance. This reminds me of a request from the United States when my first book *The Golden Bees* was published. I was sent a piece of paper, by a complete stranger, on which I was asked to write: 'For my very good friends, Marguerite and Orville'. Which I did. What the hell, they'd bought the book.

22 April 1990

A bit of advance publicity for *Napoleon and Josephine: A Love Story*, which is to be published tomorrow. I had written to the columnist, Godfrey Smith on the *Sunday Times* to say that, in all my years of research into the Napoleonic saga, I had never come across the famous expression 'Not tonight, Josephine.' Did any of his readers know its origin? He featured my request a couple of weeks ago and today, among some saltier suggestions, comes what is probably the correct one. It is a line from a play *The Royal Divorce* written by W. G. Wills in 1891.

To London tomorrow to face the launch.

24 May 1990

The frightfully grand voice on the telephone yesterday belonged to a reporter on — of all papers — the *Sun*. He is anxious to discuss the question of Napoleon's penis. The story is this. In her review of *Napoleon and Josephine* in the *Listener*, Linda Grant accused me of not knowing that Napoleon's penis had been cut off after death and was now in the hands — so to speak — of Conrad Black, proprietor of the *Telegraph*. Her claim is nonsense and I wrote to the *Listener* to say so. It is this exchange which interests the *Sun*.

I tell the reporter as much as I can which is, I suspect, not nearly enough. Certainly not spicy enough for the *Sun*. I put down the telephone, presuming that I have heard the last of it.

But this morning our friend Judy Olivier (part of whose job is to read all the newspapers) rings from London to tell me that I have 'made it to the *Sun*'. She is highly amused by this. I go across to Martin's to buy a copy. A banner headline reads: 'Who's got Napoleon's Private Parte? Boney of Contention.' The report goes on to detail, in a welter of *Sun*-speak, Franglais and double entendres, what it calls 'the Battle of the Willies'. This 'fierce debate' it says, has enlivened the normally dreary columns of 'the eggheads' magazine'. I have also, I learn, claimed that Napoleon was 'GAY and that is why he was always saying "Not tonight, Josephine."'

Whatever the report may or may not do (and I doubt if it will shift one book) it has certainly sent my stock up at Martin's. By the time I buy my copy of the *Sun*, the staff have already read it, and I am treated with great reverence. [The following week, Kevin Watson, the manager at Martin's, tells me that he saw the item in the *Sun* while lying on a beach in Portugal.]

10 September 1990

I give a talk to a group in Bedford, arranged by the local library. Afterwards, a woman comes up to introduce herself. We were at school together in Kirkwood; her name then was Joan Meiring, and we have not set eyes on one another for almost fifty years. She still has what my mother used to call 'a real Meiring face' – round, flat and good-natured.

21 October 1990

A fan is anxious to get hold of a copy of *The Golden Bees*, now long out of print. I unearth a paperback edition and today he and his wife, who are visiting the West Country, come to tea. He brings me a very grand bottle of 'Edward VII' cognac. These meetings are always awkward. I feel that I come as a disappointment to this sort of fan: I imagine that they are expecting someone grander, richer, more of 'a character'.

But things go well enough. They go even better when the wife, on hearing that I was born in South Africa, tells me that she has just read an excellent biography of Cecil Rhodes. This is, of course, Brian's book. So to her amazement — and Brian's — I call him in. Everything ends cheerfully: they have killed two birds and we have acquired a bottle of brandy.

6 December 1990

My next book is to be a study of the British royal family during the Second World War. So have written letters to the Queen Mother; Princess Margaret; Princess Alice, Duchess of Gloucester and Lord Harewood, to ask if they would share some wartime memories with me. Today brings a letter from Alistair Aird, now Sir Alastair Aird, to say that the Queen Mother has agreed to do this. Am delighted.

PART IV

'We would come home feeling quite cheered up'

The Queen Mother on the wartime spirit of the British people

London, 13 February 1991

To Clarence House to see the Queen Mother for *The Royal Family at War*. It has been snowing heavily and I slither down St James's in my entirely unsuitable black shoes. Yesterday the IRA lobbed a bomb at 10 Downing Street, and Stable Yard, outside Clarence House, is barricaded and policed. A cheery policeman knows that I am expected; he even has a blurred photograph of me taken, I assume, from the jacket of one of my books.

As Sir Alastair Aird and I go into the small drawing room on the right we find two corgis, each lying on the more comfortable of the chairs. So, not wanting to disturb them, we sit on two less comfortable ones. After a few minutes' chat, we hear the Queen Mother coming down the stairs; or rather, I hear her rapping out some orders to a member of her staff. What, I wonder, could possibly need attending to in this well-run, long-established household? (The Queen Mother, Aird tells me, hates any staff changes.)

The Queen Mother is somewhat cosily dressed for our meeting: in a white and deep-pink flowered dress with a matching deep-pink cashmere cardigan. At the age of ninety, she is as alert, vivacious and straight-backed as ever. 'Isn't it romantic!' she exclaims, with a sweeping gesture towards the snowy vista outside. Not for me, it isn't, in my wet shoes.

I start by asking her about her reaction to the outbreak of

the war. 'We were stunned,' she says. 'Sorrowful, of course, but mainly stunned.' When I broach the Munich crisis of the year before, she is disarmingly frank. 'They all complain about Chamberlain nowadays,' she says, 'but at the time he had a great deal of support. At least he gave us another year in which to get ready.' And on the question of the possible evacuation of the royal family in the event of an invasion, she is dismissive. 'It just never occurred to us; we never gave it a thought.' (If it hadn't occurred to them, it had – as I know – occurred to the government.)

Had the royal couple's celebrated visits to the bombed-out areas of the country been a harrowing experience? Her answer is unexpected. 'On the contrary,' she says, 'often we would come back from seeing the most terrible devastation feeling quite cheerful. There was something so uplifting about people's behaviour. So many times people would say to me "Ah well, no use complaining." Really, we would come home feeling quite cheered up.'

She is quoted as having once said that she always wore her best clothes when visiting the bombed-out East End, on the grounds that the East Enders would have worn their best clothes if they were visiting her. 'I just wore my old things,' she protests. She assures me, not entirely convincingly, that clothes rationing was strictly adhered to. 'Suddenly one would be told that one could only have so many buttonholes, because if one didn't, it would affect the war effort!' From this we digress to a discussion about her personal style of dressing. ('She is not chic', said the French fashion writers on her state visit to Paris in 1938, 'but she dresses like a queen.')

The door of the drawing room has been left open and the

corgis come dashing into the room and bustle around our chairs. 'Such well-behaved little ladies,' says the Queen Mother.

She tells me a strange story about a wartime intruder. In spite of the elaborate defence system around Windsor Castle, as she was dressing for dinner one evening she went into an adjoining room where she found herself confronted by a strange man. She remained quite calm. 'Putting on my best nanny voice, I told him that he had no business there and that he was to go away immediately. And he did.' What had he wanted? 'Oh, he just wanted to speak to me. People were always wanting to speak to me about something or other.'

She was one of the very few people in the country to know the true extent of the wartime casualties. 'The King was told everything so, of course, I knew everything as well. That's when I learned to keep things to myself. There were so many rumours going round at that time; one heard so many stories. I became very cagey. And I've been very cagey ever since.'

She is anxious to stress the national consensus, the coming together, the feeling of everyone 'doing their bit' during the war. 'All those bridge-playing ladies suddenly driving trucks' she comments. Her summing-up of the monarchy's contribution is modest. 'We just tried to do our best,' she says.

The interview over, Billy [Tallon] calls me into his office. He has a great pile of my books for signing. They have been sent over from Buckingham Palace. I am surprised to see that all my books, even the earliest ones like *The Golden Bees* and *Royal Vendetta*, are there.

I leave Clarence House more than ever convinced that, in

the present royal family, the Queen Mother has achieved something unique. None of the others has managed to do what she has done. The Queen is generally regarded as dutiful but dull, Prince Philip as intelligent but arrogant, Princess Margaret as colourful but imperious, Prince Charles as well-intentioned but stodgy, the Princess of Wales as glamorous but unstable, Princess Anne as conscientious but charmless, the Duchess of York as big-hearted but reckless. Only the Queen Mother, in her heyday, proved that it is possible to be a charismatic figure without ever putting a foot wrong.

Frome, 20 February 1991

A long letter today from the 'Committee for the Restoration of the Stuarts' in New York. In almost impenetrable legal jargon it sets out the thesis – I think – that as the accession of the House of Hanover to the British throne was 'contrary to Colonial law', the 'disinherited Stuarts' retained their rights in the American colonies. Taken to its ultimate, this reasoning means that the present-day Stuart pretender (an obscure Bavarian duke) is the rightful King of the United States; or rather, I imagine, of the original colonies.

'We would be interested', ends the letter, 'in your opinion as to the significance of this development.'

What 'development' exactly? Anyway, I make my reply as tactful, and as vague, as possible.

[Since then, I have been kept au fait with further, even more complicated-sounding developments.]

Cape Town, 20 April 1991

We are in Cape Town for the South African launching of Brian's *Those Bloody Women: Three Heroines of the Boer War*.

This morning he addresses a breakfast gathering of librarians and booksellers in the Netherlands Club, watched over by a portrait of Queen Beatrix. Gratifying to see a few black faces in the audience – this is, as we keep being told, the 'new South Africa'. Brian, who hates public speaking, is nervous but, once on his feet, does splendidly. Afterwards, I am asked to say a few words. I tell them about my recent interview with the Queen Mother. As tonight's *Cape Argus* puts it, I 'display no nerves'.

21 April 1991

At Joy Collier's party I meet a fan: a millionairess (many times over, I imagine) who spends the British winters in the Cape. She explains how she has recently solved a dilemma. Having sold her house in Belgravia, she didn't know where to live. 'Then I had this brilliant idea.' She moved into a self-contained suite in a hotel – Grosvenor House, Park Lane. 'It couldn't', she assures me, 'be more convenient.' I daresay.

Frome, 15 May 1991

Have been asked by the new *Dictionary of National Biography* to write entries on two of King Edward VII's mistresses: Lillie Langtry and Alice Keppel. Alice Keppel's birth certificate has proved very difficult to track down: I've tried everywhere. Finally receive a copy of it today. She was born, not in Scotland as she always asserted but in Woolwich and I'm amused to see that she was a year older than she admitted to.

10 June 1991

I am working in the top garden when a woman, passing by, asks if she may say something to me. She wants to thank me for all the years of pleasure that I have given her. Assuming that she is one of my readers, I thank her profusely. What she is referring to, however, is the yearly show of yellow roses beside the front gate.

14 June 1991

Lunch with Princess Alice, Duchess of Gloucester, at Barn-well Manor, for *The Royal Family at War*. As I drive up, just before twelve, I see the Princess, in gardening gear and straw hat, rushing into the house. Yet by the time she greets me, less than ten minutes later, she has changed her clothes and tidied her hair. Not bad for almost ninety. On an easel there is a portrait sketch of her, just completed by one of her sisters. 'It needs a few more wrinkles, a few more wrinkles,' says Betty Chalmers. The Princess ignores her.

We settle down to chat about her wartime memories. I soon realize that her physical agility is not matched by her mental. Her memory is going; only by a great deal of prompting on my part can I get any sort of sensible information out of her.

But she has one very funny story about her late husband. I daresay that she has told it many times before. Once, on returning from some foreign tour of inspection, the Duke was due to fly into an American airforce base not far from Barnwell Manor. So the Duchess – as she then was – drove over to meet his plane. On reaching the base, she was surprised and delighted to find a host of journalists and photographers also waiting for the plane. Quite clearly, she thought, the Duke's mission had been a newsworthy one. The plane landed, the Duke stepped out, and the horde of newsmen promptly disappeared. There had been a rumour that the film star, Cary Grant, was to be on the plane.

Princess Alice's son, the 46-year-old Prince Richard, Duke of Gloucester, is also at Barnwell today. He looks rather owl-like and struck me as being somewhat petulant. But as he'd just had an estimate for the rewiring of Barnwell Manor running, I imagine, into thousands of pounds, I can appreciate his mood. It must be enormously expensive to keep one very old lady and her staff in this huge house. For her to leave it, though, would break her heart.

At lunch we help ourselves to cold chicken and salads on a side table. They all eat tremendously fast. The Duke has that royal way of rapping out questions. 'Which of your books is your favourite?' he asks. I say I never know. 'Which has been the most successful?' It's *The King in Love: Edward VII's Mistresses* but I feel that I can't really tell him that: the King was his great-grandfather. The Duke drinks no stimulants: no alcohol, tea or coffee. I suppose that with a father who drank only too many stimulants, chiefly whisky, it's understandable.

During our afternoon talk, Princess Alice, who suffers back pain, shows me a special low, backless, forward-sloping chair, which is meant to help sufferers. Although there is nothing wrong with my back, I try it out. This involves locking my legs behind the front legs of the chair so that I am all but kneeling. I pretend it's very comfortable and, mainly because I can only unwind myself with difficulty, remain seated in it. When the Duke comes into the room, I feel that I have to get up and only just manage it. When he leaves, I re-lock myself. But then he keeps coming in and going out of the room, and instead of telling me not to get up each time, he leaves me to battle on like some demented jack-in-the-box. I suppose that, in that royal way, he doesn't even notice. But he should, he is years younger than me.

The three of us have tea together, round a little table laid in the drawing room. The Princess and I drink tea; the Duke drinks milk; we all eat crumpets. Although so reserved, Princess Alice has a way of keeping the conversation going; the better I know her, the more I admire her. I leave after tea and pick Brian up in Oundle, where he has had his hair cut.

28 June 1991

Get a telephone call from a man living in Germany who is convinced that the World Wildlife Fund is a sinister organization set on world domination. The chief plotters, apparently, are the Duke of Edinburgh and Prince Bernhard of the Netherlands. The caller seems to interpret even minor domestic upsets in the royal family as further proof of the machinations of Prince Philip: they are all, it seems, part of

his master plan to convert the World Wildlife Fund into
some sort of global government.

Or that, at least, is what I think he means.

12 July 1991

Am told a good story which I will be able to use in the
book. It illustrates Field-Marshal Montgomery's well-known
vanity. During the war, each Tuesday, Churchill would lunch
with King George VI at Buckingham Palace. One Tuesday
the two men were discussing Montgomery. 'I'm very worried
about Monty; I think he's after my job,' said Churchill.
'Thank God,' said the King. 'I thought he was after mine.'

31 July 1991

To Kensington Palace for lunch with Princess Margaret for
The Royal Family at War. The train is on time and even though
I walk all the way from Paddington Station to the Palace, I
am early. So I sit in the little covered way beside St Mary
Abbots, on the corner of High and Church Streets. I was last
here ten years ago for the memorial service for Princess Alice,
Countess of Athlone. As always before these royal interviews,
I feel vaguely apprehensive.

As I cross the Palace courtyard towards Princess Margaret's door, I see her chef lounging in another doorway,
smoking a cigarette. The walls of HRH's downstairs cloakroom are lined with framed addresses of welcome and
freedoms of cities. Did all those painstaking calligraphers ever
imagine that their handiwork would end up here?

The Princess quickly switches off what sounds like Radio Three when I am announced. She is dressed in bright yellow and wears a great deal of jewellery. (She once admitted to having no casual clothes; she always dresses as though for a public appearance.) She looks, these days, more like her father, the late King George VI: hers is a feminine version of his lined, sensitive, wide-mouthed face. She still has a certain sexual allure and her manner remains half-approachable, half-imperious.

Princess Margaret was just nine when the Second World War broke out and almost fifteen when it ended. ('Who is this Hitler, spoiling everything?' she famously demanded, on hearing that the royal family's annual Balmoral holiday was likely to be cancelled in the autumn of 1939 because of the worsening political situation.) Her memories of the five wartime years spent in Windsor Castle are vivid. She is dismissive of the precautions taken to safeguard the family. 'They would never have kept the Germans out,' she says, 'but they certainly kept us in.'

Hitler, she tells me, planned to make Windsor Castle his headquarters once Britain had been conquered. Only after the war was she told that arrangements had been made to spirit the royal family away in the event of a German invasion. A series of suitable houses had been chosen as possible places of refuge. 'There was a line of them,' she tells me, 'we were to be shunted from one to the other until we reached Liverpool.' From there they would sail to Canada. At the time she knew nothing about this. 'We were never told *anything.*'

On the Princess's occasional wartime journeys to or

through London, she was always surprised at how much of the capital had not been flattened. 'We had heard so much about the bombs that I had expected everything to be destroyed. There was really quite a lot standing.' Royal wartime rationing (which I suspect was an exercise in example-setting rather than a necessity) has left her with a horror of waste: of people who 'plaster their bread with butter'.

Over lunch (rissoles, wine for me and lots of Famous Grouse for HRH) the Princess comes out with some typically idiosyncratic remarks. Before the Clean Air Act, she assures me, she had to wipe every single leaf of her camellias by hand. It is a diverting picture. I tell her how much the New Look of the late 1940s and early 1950s used to suit her. She agrees. 'When I met Mr Dior in Paris,' she drawls, 'I thanked him so much for creating the New Look.' One would imagine that he had created it especially for her. She refers to her grandfather, King George V, as 'a most objectionable old man'.

I don't, of course, mention the present domestic upheavals in the royal family. I know that her previously warm relationship with the Princess of Wales has cooled; and that she regards the Duchess of York as beyond the pale. But she is obviously grateful that the once-merciless media spotlight has now swung away from her. 'They leave me alone these days,' she says. 'They've got other fish to fry.'

15 August 1991

To Ewelme, a village near Oxford, for my meeting with Viscountess Hambledon, who was once Lady of the Bed-chamber to Queen Elizabeth, now the Queen Mother. (The title, she explains, meant that she was more than a lady-in-waiting: she accompanied the Queen only when the King was present.) Lady Hambledon is a tall, aristocratic, still-handsome woman in her eighties. Lunch, at a table set under the trees, is served by one of the new breed of upper-class girls (this one in baggy shorts) who cook for the likes of Lady Hambledon.

Discreet about the royal family, Lady Hambledon is outspoken about everything else. She is scathing about Margaret Thatcher ('corrupted by power') and the iniquities of the poll tax. 'I'm a wealthy woman', she says, 'and my char pays exactly the same tax as I do. It's ridiculous.'

She is interesting about King George VI's stammer. 'It was always worse indoors. Once he was in the open air, it tended to disappear.' She comes out with the official line on the late King. It was he, and not the Queen, who made all the important decisions, she insists. 'He was a man of very sound judgement. The Queen always relied on him. Before coming to any decision or even accepting an invitation, she would always say, "I'll have to ask the King."'

There is more evidence of the official line when, out of the blue, Lady Hambledon suddenly announces that the Queen Mother is not at all interested in clothes. I wonder why she has brought this up. It appears that she has recently spent a weekend as the Queen Mother's guest. She had apparently told the Queen Mother that she was due to see me in connection with my book and, just as apparently, the Queen Mother had told her that she was afraid that I may have come away from our recent meeting with the impression that she was deeply interested in clothes. I suspect that she has asked Lady Hambledon to correct this impression. I suppose the Queen Mother doesn't want to be seen as extravagant. So Lady Hambledon now makes a point of assuring me that the Queen Mother is 'not interested in clothes at all'.

Only once does Lady Hambledon's discretion desert her. She had accompanied the Queen Mother and Princess Margaret on their tour of Rhodesia in 1953. It was during this tour that the Queen Mother had the painful task of telling her daughter that Peter Townsend – the Queen Mother's comptroller with whom the Princess was deeply in love, but who, as a divorced man, was a highly unsuitable choice – would not be at home to greet her on her return to London: his exile to Brussels had been deliberately brought forward. The effect on the Princess was dramatic. For the following four days she vanished from public view. The official explanation was that the Princess had succumbed to a bout of 'Bulawayo flu' and had been flown to Salisbury to recover. The other version – that she staged a scene, lapsed into a sulk and refused to continue the tour – seems, on balance, to be the more likely. Lady Hambledon's testimony seems to confirm this. 'I was there when Princess Margaret was told about the Peter Townsend business,' she tells me. 'It was *not* very pleasant.'

7 September 1991

I am contacted by an American television company. A black actor, of whom I have never heard, has just published a book in which he claims to be a direct descendant of King Edward VII. The King, when Prince of Wales, was visiting Nigeria where he had sex with the actor's grandmother (or is it great-grandmother?) who was a princess and who subsequently bore him a son. Was I prepared to be interviewed about this? For a fee, yes. I make clear, however, that as the future King Edward VII never set foot in Nigeria, I regard the whole story as nonsense.

The team arrives with the usual mountain of equipment and proceeds to move the furniture about. I do my piece and they then announce that they want some footage of me walking around Frome. To the bewilderment of passers-by, I am shot walking up our chief tourist attraction – Cheap Street – and then dodging the cars in the Market Place.

[Weeks later, an American friend rings to say that he has seen the interview in which this three-storeyed house in a busy street is described as 'a quaint old English cottage' and Frome – with its banks, building societies, estate agents, solicitors' offices and snarled-up traffic – as 'a typical little English village'.]

London, 5 May 1992

I go to see Lord Harewood for *The Royal Family at War*. He has recently moved from his house in Little Venice to a flat in Maida Vale. He now sports a beard which makes his resemblance to his late mother [King George V's only daughter] less noticeable. I congratulate him on the flat, which is very spacious. The downstairs entrance hall, he complains, is 'very grotty'.

We talk about his wartime experiences, particularly his imprisonment in Colditz. As one of the so-called prominenti – being King George VI's nephew he was especially valuable to the Germans – he was at greater risk than the other prisoners. But he was never, he says, particularly apprehensive. 'Fear is a sterile emotion,' he claims. Throughout his captivity he had never, for instance, had any trouble falling asleep: the mind, he maintains, 'puts up its own defences'.

I tell him that I have already seen the Queen Mother for my book. At this his eyes glaze over. I suspect that there is little love lost between the two of them. Harewood's divorce from his first wife – rendered more 'scandalous' by the fact that he had by then already fathered a child by a divorcee who was to become his second wife – is said to have annoyed the Queen Mother. Her alleged disapproval led to a prolonged period of coolness towards Harewood in the royal family.

After I have been with him for about an hour, Lord Harewood picks up a clock on his desk and begins, very slowly and deliberately, to wind it. I take the hint and clear off.

Frome, 20 May 1992

We go to the Theatre Royal, Bath, to see a matinee of *The Madness of George III* by Alan Bennett. Excellent. Nigel Hawthorne plays the King and gets a standing ovation. After the show we meet him for tea at the Francis Hotel. Nigel and I were at the University of Cape Town together: he at the drama school, I at·the art school. We were often in plays together — he the lead and I lucky to get a few lines.

In those days we all thought that another young actor, Jobie Stewart, would be the one to make a name for himself. Nigel seemed too stodgy; he had none of Jobie's dash. When Nigel and Jobie arrived in Britain in 1951, Ted Darroll and I, who had arrived a couple of months before, went to meet them off the boat train from Southampton. Soon after that, Nigel disappeared from my life for many years: not until I saw him in *Yes, Minister* did I realize that his time had come, that his long years of battling in this most difficult of professions were over.

The awkward, unresolved student is now an urbane, self-assured and very famous actor. He treats the waitress, who is all a-flutter at serving 'Sir Humphrey', with a practised charm.

We talk about Gwen Ffrangcon-Davies. In our young days, she often appeared, with her friend Marda Vanne, on the South African stage. I once even played a scene with her. Nigel still sees her from time to time. I remember a story, which Gwen once told the actress Vivienne Drummond, concerning the royal visit to South Africa in 1947. As Gwen and Marda happened to be in Pretoria at the same time as

King George VI and Queen Elizabeth, they were invited to have a drink with the royal couple at Government House. Gwen who, unlike Marda, was always very dressy, was wearing a pair of elbow-length white gloves but, just before the royal couple came into the room, she suddenly decided that the gloves had been a mistake. She stripped them off, rolled them into a ball and shoved them under the cushion of her chair. The greetings over, the Queen seated herself in the chair in which Gwen had been sitting. Feeling a lump under the cushion, she drew out the gloves. 'Oh, here they are,' said the Queen to the King. And Gwen Ffrangcon-Davies never saw her gloves again.

11 June 1992

We drive to the Royal Archives at Windsor Castle, to choose illustrations for *The Royal Family at War*. As always, Frances Dimond, the curator of the Royal Photographic Collection, is helpful and efficient. She shows us her outsize tricycle on which she pedals to work every day. I find a photograph of King George VI and Queen Elizabeth on the Buckingham Palace balcony on VJ Day, with the Queen wearing, for the first time, one of those elaborate hats that were to become her hallmark for the following four decades. It could make a good jacket illustration. [It didn't. John Murray preferred one of the royal couple amid the rubble of a bombed Buckingham Palace.]

Afterwards, we go to St George's Chapel because I want to see the tomb of Prince Albert Victor, Duke of Clarence. I have always been drawn, in my writing, to lost causes: to fallen thrones, exiles, pretenders, might-have-beens. The Duke of Clarence, Queen Victoria's grandson and, as the eldest son of the future King Edward VII, heir to the British throne, was one of the royal family's great conundrums. He died, aged twenty-eight, in 1892. An air of mystery has always surrounded the Duke of Clarence – known, in the family, as Eddy. He was a curious creature: apathetic, immature, unresolved. His name has been associated with two great Victorian scandals. It has been claimed that he was Jack the Ripper; a claim that is patently nonsense. And he is rumoured to have been involved in the famous homosexual brothel case – the Cleveland Street Scandal. I have always thought that there are firmer grounds for this second accusation.

It is many years since I last saw his tomb: an art nouveau masterpiece by Sir Alfred Gilbert. But when we get to the Albert Memorial Chapel, the Victorian annex to St George's Chapel, we find that it is closed. All my enquiries are met by that maddening sort of shoulder shrugging: no one seems to know why it is closed or for how long it will be closed. We leave disappointed.

By the time we reach Frome after our long drive back, I have decided that my next book will be a life of Prince Eddy; or rather, an exploration into his life.

30 June 1992

A Frenchwoman telephones this evening. Could I explain the rise and fall of the British Empire to her? She would like it explained now, over the telephone. I suggest she read a book on the subject.

23 July 1992

The BBC (Radio) is preparing obituaries of various members of the royal family and I have agreed to speak about the Queen Mother. Today the woman comes to record me; rather ghoulish, and I keep forgetting to speak in the past tense.

9 December 1992

The phone going all day. The announcement that Charles and Diana have agreed to separate has brought a flurry of requests for radio and television interviews. Goodness know why: I know little more than anyone else. I refuse to go all the way to London so, in the end, a car is sent from BBC Bristol from where I am linked up to London for various programmes. Wish I'd had my hair cut last week.

26 January 1993

A Japanese television company has been on to me for weeks to work on a programme on 'royal ghost stories'. I don't want to do it as I am far too busy researching my Prince Eddy book. Finally, on my agent Andrew Lownie's advice, I demand an enormous fee. This does the trick. They ring today to say that they are abandoning – or, rather, postponing – the project.

30 April 1993

Have been asked to take part in a discussion on the future of the monarchy by a new cable-television station, based in Bristol. Also invited is Yvone Sterenborg, a dedicated monarchist, living in Frome. A car fetches us and we arrive at a scene of complete chaos. A restaurant has been taken over for the night and the tables are filled with a crowd of inarticulate youngsters. The 'discussion' is little more than a sustained diatribe against the monarchy, with Yvone and me hardly getting a word in.

This is followed by an equally incoherent discussion on contraception. As Yvone Sterenborg was a nurse, she has some contribution to make; I have none. The whole shambolic evening ends merrily, with free condoms being handed out to everyone present.

[We later discover that the whole thing had been a trial run, and never released.]

20 May 1993

Publication day for *The Royal Family at War* brings two letters about my last book, *Napoleon and Josephine*. Both are from Germany. One is a handsome cheque from the German publishers of the paperback [*Napoleon and Josephine* was published in nine languages] and the other is a query from a woman doctor. In the German translation, she tells me, Josephine's dog is described as a 'boxer'; surely he was a pug? I assure her that Josephine's dog, Fortuné (who bit

Napoleon in the leg on his wedding night) was indeed a pug.

London, 27 May 1993

We are spending ten days in London, staying in my niece Sue Manby's flat just off Holland Road. She is away, in her house in Provence. I am killing two birds: doing publicity for *The Royal Family at War* and research for *Prince Eddy*.

Today, as we are walking through the Embankment Gardens, a young Japanese woman comes up to ask us the way to Buckingham Palace. I explain how to get there on the Underground; she wants to go there, she says, 'to see Princess Diana'. I tell her that the Princess lives in Kensington Palace and that she will have to take the Tube to High Street Kensington. Will she be able, she asks, to go into the palace to visit the Princess? Not without an appointment, I tell her. How can she make an appointment? I explain that it would be all but impossible to do so. She bursts into tears. She has come all the way from Japan especially to see 'Princess Diana'. She thinks that she is 'the most wonderful person in the world'. There has never been a person in 'the history' like 'Princess Diana'.

I feel helpless in the face of this tearful adoration. Cravenly, I suggest that she go to Kensington Palace and ask 'the policeman' if it will be possible for her to see the Princess. She must ask him to tell the Princess that she has come all the way from Japan. Who knows? With Diana, it might just work. The girl cheers up and heads for Charing Cross Underground station.

28 May 1993

This evening we go for a drink in a nearby pub called The Duke of Clarence. I had presumed that the name referred to the Duke of Clarence who became King William IV. But, on going in, we discover that the walls are crowded with pictures of *my* Duke of Clarence – Prince Eddy. Serendipity? But it's odd, as he's such a forgotten figure. I don't imagine that anyone, either drinking or serving, in the pub, has the slightest idea who he was.

Cambridge, 29 June 1993

We are in beautiful Cambridge, staying in Churchill College, where I am working in the archives on the Esher papers. Lord Esher was a close friend of Lord Arthur Somerset – the man who was accused of having frequented the male brothel in Cleveland Street in the late 1880s. The case against Somerset was mysteriously dropped when it was alleged that a 'very distinguished person' was also implicated in the affair. This person was almost certainly Prince Eddy, heir to the British throne. Today, in the letters between Lord Esher and Lord Arthur Somerset (both men were gay), I come across what seems to be irrefutable proof that Prince Eddy was indeed involved. It's like finding the final piece in a jigsaw puzzle. And it's what makes researching and writing – even if only now and then – such a rewarding business.

15 August 1993

In the course of disproving the absurd claim that Prince Eddy was Jack the Ripper, I have become very interested in the whole Ripper mystery. The chief suspect, at the time and since, is a man called Montague John Druitt. He was born in Wimborne, Dorset and, after his heavily weighted body was fished out of the Thames, buried there.

Today Brian and I drive down to Wimborne in search of Druitt's grave. At the local tourist office we are met by blank looks. So we scour the cemeteries and eventually find the graves of Montague Druitt and his brother William beside an Anglican chapel. Just two simple crosses, beneath one of which lies, quite probably, the answer to one of the great riddles of the past century.

27 January 1994

A telephone call from a television producer named Joffe who is planning to make a documentary on the royal family during the Second World War. (Some months ago he gave me coffee at the BAFTA headquarters in London.) He wants to know if I would be prepared to interview the Queen Mother for his programme. I agree, provided I don't have to make the approach. I also tell him that it is extremely unlikely that she would ever agree to be interviewed. In fact, there's not a cat in hell's chance that she would. [This was the last that I ever heard of the project.]

I February 1994

With every new twist in the on-going saga of the Wales's marriage, I am contacted by radio and television stations. Although I know very little about it other than what I read in the press, I am by now adept at pontificating on the situation, and come across as very assured and knowledgeable.

Most interviewers assume that one is either 'pro-Charles' or 'pro-Diana' or, even more simplistic, that all men are for Charles and all women for Diana. I never cease to be astounded by how strongly the callers-in on these radio programmes feel about the whole business. My pontifications are as nothing compared to the confidence with which these callers lay down the law on the subject. 'Why can't they just leave them alone?' is the usual plaintive cry. As though the break-up of the royal marriage is entirely due to media intrusion.

Am sometimes tempted to announce, on air, that I couldn't give a stuff either way.

Chaos this morning when a BBC television team arrive to do yet another interview on the subject. They are due at ten. At a quarter to ten Brian is busy putting away some books in the front hall when the doorbell rings. Anxious to get out of the way before they come in, he dashes out, catches his foot in the flex of the brass table lamp and brings the lamp crashing down, shattering the chimney of the lamp and its white glass globe. At that moment the telephone rings. Brian clears off, I answer the telephone, tell the caller to hang on, open the door, and the television team, loaded down with equipment, have to pick their way over the broken glass.

[The hour-long interview is cut down to a few minutes on the evening news.]

18 February 1994

A telephone call today from a woman wanting 'additional' information on Alice Keppel. I tell her that I put everything I know into my book (*The King in Love*). Had she read it? She admits that she hasn't. I suggest that she do so and hang up. We suspect that she is a journalist, wanting to make the connection between Alice Keppel and Camilla Parker Bowles.

4 June 1994

Each time I've seen the Queen Mother, we've talked about South Africa. She deeply regrets its break with the Commonwealth or, more especially I suspect, the break with the monarchy. 'We were a bridge,' she says, with a neat hand gesture; meaning that the monarchy acts as the connecting link between Britain and the members of the Commonwealth. Like her daughter, Queen Elizabeth II, the Queen Mother sees the monarchy's Commonwealth role as a highly significant one. (The Commonwealth emerged from the Empire and the Queen Mother is, of course, the last Empress of India.)

And so, with South Africa having rejoined the Commonwealth after the change of regime and the inauguration of

Nelson Mandela, I wrote to the Queen Mother to say how delighted I am that the 'bridge' has been restored. Today brings an answer from Sir Alastair Aird to say how 'very touched' the Queen Mother has been by my letter. One never knows, of course, whether this is simply diplomatic language: in this case, I suspect not.

The same post brings a letter for Brian to say that his only 'royal' book — *The Zulu Kings* — is to have a new American edition.

2 July 1994

The *Daily Sport* has somehow got hold of an advance copy of my *Prince Eddy and the Homosexual Underworld*, and, under the banner headline 'Prince Eddy and the Old Queens', launches into a mass of double entendres along the lines of the Queen not being amused by claims that Prince Eddy is a 'raving woofter' — without making clear that 'the Queen' is Queen Victoria and 'Prince Eddy' her grandson, the Duke of Clarence.

London, 20 July 1994

We have been allotted seats in Westminster Abbey for the service to mark the welcoming back of South Africa into the Commonwealth. The Queen Mother is to attend. It is a boiling hot day (I always forget how hot London can be in the summer) and we are in dark suits. The congregation is full of wonderful old exiles; we recognize several faces from the banned South Africa Liberal Party of the 1950s.

The Queen Mother arrives in one of her standard summer outfits of matching dress, coat and hat – this time in white and green. She is clearly in agony from her hip and uses a stick, but she converts every grimace of pain into a tight smile and, magnificent old trouper that she is, battles her way right up the length of the nave.

Archbishop Tutu is at his expansive best. 'This is a right ROYAL occasion,' he declaims, 'in the present of a Q-U-E-E-N.' Although I very much doubt that this particular Queen welcomes the end of White rule in South Africa.

I find it all intensely moving. And when the congregation sings the national anthems – 'God Save the Queen', 'Nkosi Sikelel I Afrika' and even 'Die Stem' – I break up and have to keep my eyes fixed firmly on my shoes.

Frome, 27 August 1994

During the last few years several of my earlier books have been reprinted in paperback: *Grandmama of Europe, Victoria and Disraeli, Kings over the Water, Princess Alice.* Now Paul Minet, who runs Piccadilly Rare Books and produces a monthly magazine called *Royalty Digest*, has started a series of hardback reprints. He wants to do a reprint of *Royal Vendetta: The Crown of Spain 1829–1965.* I'm delighted about this.

If I do have a favourite out of all my books, I think that *Royal Vendetta* must come pretty high on the list. For one thing the action covers a turbulent period in Spanish history, full of colourful characters and tumultuous events. For another, research entailed a five-month-long stay in Spain. In the spring of 1965 Brian and I sailed from South Africa to

Britain where we took delivery of a new car – a Mini which overheated and whose battery had to be topped up at least twice a day – and drove down through France and into Spain. For the following five months we travelled throughout that fascinating country; made more fascinating by the fact that our journey had a specific purpose – research. We then drove on to Trieste where the self-styled Carlist Kings of Spain were buried. From there we sailed back, with the overheating Mini on board, down the East African coast to South Africa.

Some years later, on another visit to Europe, we sailed into Barcelona where our Spanish publishers, Grijalbo, were head-quartered. They had published Brian's *The Diamond Magnates* and my *The Golden Bees* and, of course, *Royal Vendetta*. We were met on the quayside by a youngish man called Vivas who managed Grijalbo. In our jeans and with our suntans we obviously looked younger than he had imagined we would be (we were in our late thirties at that stage). 'I was expecting two old professors,' he said. So, changing plans, he took us to a funfair, where we went on the big dipper and where he bought us ice-creams. We didn't look *that* young. He did, however, give us a wonderful lunch, starting at three and ending at five.

London, 20 September 1994

The always efficient and enthusiastic Robin Piguet, at Hatchard's, has arranged for me to sign copies of *Prince Eddy and the Homosexual Underworld*. Thank goodness it's not a public signing session. They can be torture. There you sit, pretending to be absorbed in your own book and not a soul comes near you.

Once, in a department store, I was signing copies of *Grandmama of Europe*. I was sitting there, with great piles of books on either side of me and a banner above me, when a woman, assuming that I was manning the information desk, asked if I knew the way to the grocery department. The manager of the book department dashed up and, thrusting a copy of the book into the woman's hands, explained that I was the 'eminent' author, Theo Aronson, and that I was kindly signing copies of my new book. The woman looked at the book, looked at me, and said, 'So you don't know the way to the grocery department, then.'

Frome, 22 September 1994

My nephew, Nick Manby, sends me a copy of a late Victorian photograph taken of the staff of Beardmore and Company, Ironmongers, outside their premises in Cleveland Street, not far from the famous homosexual brothel in *Prince Eddy*. There they stand, this row of moustached young men in their ties, suits and ankle-length aprons, oblivious – one presumes – of the scandalous comings and goings up the road.

Nick now works for Beardmore's, which has become considerably grander since those days. He does something incomprehensible with computers.

9 October 1994

Prince Eddy has had major coverage, the strangest being the review by Kenneth Rose in the *Literary Review*. He is clearly shocked by the book which he feels sure libraries will 'keep under the counter and disgorge with reluctance'. He describes as 'bizarre practices' such things as 'masturbation, fellatio, penetration and emissions'. How else, then, does Kenneth Rose imagine people perform sexual acts? He apparently considers it 'impertinent' that I should subject even a long-dead member of the royal family to such 'undignified' treatment. And the fact that a Prince of the Blood might have been involved in homosexual goings-on is apparently unthinkable. 'The young man cannot even have a touch of fever', grumbles Rose, 'without Aronson speculating that it must have been a gonorrhoeal infection.' (It was not speculation: I gave a source for my information.)

Well, a few weeks later I was contacted by a Jim Hanson, who is a dealer in, among other things, royal correspondence. He has recently bought two letters, in Prince Eddy's own hand, in which the young man is asking his doctor for a further supply of medication to treat his recurring 'gleet', which was a Victorian term for gonorrhoea.

Today, we drive down to Devon to see Jim Hanson and there, pasted into a large leather-bound album, are Prince Eddy's two letters. He kindly gives me photostats.

I toy with the idea of writing to the *Literary Review* about my find but, in the end, decide against it.

24 October 1994

Another nutty telephone call this evening, this time from an American journalist in Germany. He has just finished reading *Prince Eddy*, which has apparently confirmed him in his suspicions that there is some sort of left-wing conspiracy against the 'free world'. The entire 'Western system' is now on the point of collapse; the monarchy doomed; capitalism in its death throes; the monetary system tottering.

What the hell all this has to do with poor Prince Eddy visiting a male brothel in 1889 is, to say the least, obscure.

I make suitably sympathetic noises, hoping he'll ring off so that I can get back to *Coronation Street*.

PART V

'Nowadays, they've got other fish to fry'

Princess Margaret on her battle with the media

Frome, 16 March 1995

AM GIVEN LUNCH, in a good Spanish restaurant, by David Roberts, who is a partner in the publishing house of Michael O'Mara. [Michael O'Mara published Andrew Morton's amazingly successful book on Diana, Princess of Wales.] Roberts is a very nice man, urbane and civilized. O'Mara want me to write a life of Princess Margaret. Although I am not really happy writing about living people, Princess Margaret is the one member of the present royal family who really interests me. She is so different from the rest of them: less county, more sophisticated, more hedonistic. It could be a fascinating book to write.

By the time lunch is over, and I have downed my half of a bottle of wine, I have agreed to write a short, page-long synopsis.

4 April 1995

After further discussion with David Roberts, I have decided to write an *unauthorized* life of the Princess. I daresay she would have co-operated with me if approached, but then one can so easily end up with a bland, uncritical, sycophantic study with no sort of bite to it. This way, I feel free to say exactly what I like and I hope that, as a result, the book will be a more honest, impartial and rounded piece of work. She is a very controversial figure and an authorized life wouldn't have brought this out.

So, it's back to the desk for the next eighteen months.

6 June 1995

Prince Charles is visiting Frome today; don't exactly know why but he goes to see our local white elephant – the handsome Rook Lane Chapel, for which no satisfactory use can ever be found. It's interesting to see the professional way in which he handles the crowds; bantering, laughing, feigning interest. But he is losing what looks he once had. He has a long, worried, very Mountbatten face but without the handsomeness of his father or his late great-uncle, Lord Louis Mountbatten. In fact, the good looks which characterized the last two generations of the royal family have gone. I daresay Diana's sons will revive them. Prince Charles also looks curiously old-fashioned and fogeyish, not at all like a young-ish man, still in his forties. His suntan is suspiciously deep; surely not the result of *this* spring's sunshine.

I remember seeing King George VI in the year before he died, attending some ceremony in Westminster Abbey. He looked well enough from a distance but, close to, one could see that he was covered in what was then known as 'pancake' make-up, with his cheeks rouged. The poor man was very ill and this presentation of himself was understandable: it was all part of kingship.

12 August 1995

Mention to anyone above a certain age that you are writing a book about Princess Margaret and they are bound to say, 'They should have let her marry Townsend.'

At the time Princess Margaret's famous renunciation of Peter Townsend was seen as a noble sacrifice. Conscious of the teachings of the Church on divorce and of her own obligations to the Crown, Princess Margaret gave up the idea of marrying Townsend. In the choice between love and duty, she chose duty. That, at least, is how the public saw it.

The more I delve into the Townsend business, the more convinced I become that the general perception of the affair is false. The Princess's choice was not between love and duty but between her life as a princess and life as Mrs Peter Townsend. If she had persisted in marrying the divorced Townsend, the government of the day would have passed a bill stripping her of all her rights, privileges and income. She would have had to be married abroad in a civil ceremony and would have been obliged to lived out of the country, on Townsend's salary. That was the real choice.

So in the end, it was not so much that the Princess sacrificed her love for Townsend for the sake of Church, Crown and Commonwealth, as that she was not prepared to sacrifice her luxurious style of life. Even so, for a young woman in love, it could not have been an easy choice.

A generation later, the marriage of Princess Margaret's divorced niece, Princess Anne, to an equerry, raised hardly a ripple of public disapproval.

Brussels, 15 September 1995

We are spending a few days in Brussels. It gives me a welcome break after months at the desk. I haven't been here for years, not since researching *The Coburgs of Belgium* in the late 1960s. Today we visit the Musée de la Dynastie in the Royal Palace. It has been considerably expanded and improved since last I saw it, with a room dedicated to each of the monarchs. Fascinating. It takes me back to the early days of my writing career. *The Coburgs of Belgium* sold very well and had four printings: one of them ten years after publication. I doubt if any publisher would consider such a book today. [It was reprinted, by Paul Minet, the following year.]

Frome, 21 November 1995

The Princess of Wales's televised interview last night keeps me on the telephone all day. The first call comes just after seven this morning. Since then, I give something like a dozen interviews. They all ask the same questions, and I give them all the same answers. In the middle of an interview with Talk Radio an elderly neighbour knocks at the door and even though Brian skilfully shepherds her away, I find myself on a sort of autopilot. Not that anyone would notice.

27 November 1995

My cranky American journalist in Germany telephones again. His conspiracy theory — of a left-wing, anti-capitalist plot —

has been strengthened by the Diana interview. It was all arranged, he assures me, by 'the Thatcherites', who are intent on 'bringing down the monarchy'. The mind boggles.

28 November 1995

A BBC television producer comes to lunch today. He is planning a programme to mark the 100th anniversary of Queen Victoria's Diamond Jubilee, which will fall in the summer of 1997. I drive to Westbury to meet his train, I give him lunch with wine, I drive him back to Westbury and I give him the benefit of my knowledge on the subject. I bet that I don't even get a thank-you note. [I don't. That is the last I hear of him. By now I really should know better.]

20 February 1996

Father Lawrence of Downside Abbey, whom we met through our friend Sandy Walford, telephones this evening to say how delighted he was to discover that I am the author of the book which is being read out, nightly, to their community. It is *Grandmama of Europe*. He has only just made the connection.

He wants to know the title of my most recent book. I have to do some quick thinking. I really can't see *Prince Eddy and the Homosexual Underworld* being read out to the assembled priests. I tell him that I am writing a life of Princess Margaret, although there are aspects of *that* lady's life that won't be suitable for ecclesiastical ears either.

29 February 1996

The news that the Princess of Wales has agreed to a divorce has meant two chaotic days for me. Telephone interviews begin last night, and from just after seven this morning I am at it almost continuously. This evening a car comes for us from the HTV studios in Bristol. From there I am linked up to London and, together with a divorce lawyer and the journalist, James Whitaker, I am launched into a discussion on the divorce. Feel totally inadequate as I have neither the lawyer's legal knowledge nor Whitaker's fund of royal gossip. In any case, with Whitaker in full and confident flow, I get very little opportunity to say anything. Nor am I helped by the fact that I was given the most vicious haircut yesterday and that I can see my almost bald head pictured in literally dozens of television monitors banked around the studio.

Brian loyally assures me that I was 'on excellent form' and after a party of wine and snacks we are driven home.

9 March 1996

Andrew Lownie telephones to say that a Polish publisher wants to publish *Royal Vendetta, Crowns in Conflict* and *Napoleon and Josephine*. The fall of communism has certainly led to a rise of interest in my work: already I have been published in Hungary and Czechoslovakia. I suppose that these countries have been starved of the sort of colourful, romantic and, above all, royal historical studies such as I write.

19 March 1996

Last autumn an independent television producer called Alan
Scales – very relaxed and professional – came to interview
me for a documentary series he is making on the royal family.
Titled *Behind Palace Walls*, it has obviously been distributed
throughout the English-speaking world. I get calls from
friends in this country and letters from friends in the United
States, Australia and South Africa, telling me that they have
seen me. We, apparently, are the only people not to have
seen it. For one thing, I didn't know the title and, for
another, the series is broadcast, in this country, on Sunday
afternoons, when we never watch television.

Am amused by how many people pretend not to watch
Sunday afternoon television. They invariably happen to be
passing through a room on their way to do something
important when they notice me on the screen. Or they are in
the kitchen preparing a meal when they recognize my voice.
Or their mothers, or their children, see me.

19 April 1995

I give a talk to a women's group in Bath. In the course of the
last few years I've noticed a change of attitude – in this sort
of audience, at least – towards the royal family. People are
still very interested in them (indeed, more so) but they are
less reverential: they are more jocular, more flippant, more
ready to criticize. It is, of course, the various royal matrimo-
nial upheavals that are responsible for this change. Except for

the always colourful love life of the ineffable Princess Margaret, the royal family has, in the recent past, been relatively free of scandal. Now it is engulfed in nothing but. The royals have revealed themselves as no different from, and certainly no better than, many other families. The catalogue of divorces, extra-marital affairs and unseemly public bickering has stripped away most of the royal mystique. Even the Queen is regarded – rightly or wrongly – as an inadequate parent. One member of today's audience even asks if I think that the monarchy will last into the coming century.

Of course it will. The monarchy has been through these troughs before. I am sure that when, in 2002, Queen Elizabeth II celebrates her Golden Jubilee, everyone will be out in the streets, cheering.

But there are still some who blame the present mess on the media. If the newspapers had 'just left them alone' the entire royal family would be living, one presumes, in a state of conjugal bliss.

London, 24 April 1996

Lunch with David Roberts and Nicholas Courtney at Brooks's in St James's. Nicholas Courtney used to work for Colin Tennant (now Lord Glenconner) who owned the island of Mustique on which Princess Margaret has her famous – some say infamous – holiday home. It was Courtney who, together with Tennant and the Princess's one-time companion, Roddy Llewellyn, was photographed nude, by Princess Margaret, on the beach on Mustique. Somehow or other, the photograph of the Princess's three male friends, unmistakably naked, found its way into the *News of the World*. The incident hardly improved her already shaky reputation.

Nicholas Courtney tells me a charming story. When Princess Margaret's house on Mustique (paid for by Colin Tennant's company) was complete, her furniture arrived from London in a vast wooden container which took all day to unload. By that same evening the empty container had been converted into a home by an impoverished island family. Windows had been cut into the sides and a verandah, roofed in palm fronds, added. On the sides of the 'house' there remained stencilled, in bold black letters, the words 'HRH Princess Margaret'.

After lunch I go to Hatchard's where Robin Piguet has set out great piles of the paperback of *Prince Eddy* for signing. Soon, the achievement will be to find an *unsigned* copy of the book.

This evening I return to Hatchard's for their Authors of the Year party to which I am always invited. Sometimes I wander dolefully about, desperate to find a familiar face. But this evening I begin chatting, almost immediately, to Beryl Bainbridge, Bernice Rubens and Francis King. He tells the other two how he and I first met almost thirty-five years ago when, armed with his telephone number given to me by Felicity Mason whom I bumped into in Rome, I arrived in Athens, where he was working for the British Council. I was then on my Napoleonic pilgrimage: that six-month-long hitch-hike from Ostend in Belgium to Port Elizabeth in South Africa.

Francis King was still an unpublished writer in those days (and so, most certainly, was I), and it was only years later, on coming across my diary for that period, that I realized that the man I had known in Athens was the same Francis King whose books I now read so avidly. A feature of those days, which now strikes me as bizarre, was how often I would bump into people I knew in the streets of cities like Rome and Florence and Venice. Unthinkable today.

Later I chat to Lady Longford. By now there is such a din that only by shouting into her right ear can I make myself heard. She asks how my book on Princess Margaret is coming along. We discuss the difficulties of writing about people who are still alive; particularly so in the case of Princess Margaret. Well, says Lady Longford, with a wealth of meaning, 'She has always been very good to *me*.'

Frome, 10 May 1996

I visit Hugo Vickers, newly married and who now lives in the country in great style in the house that belonged to his late father. He gives me lunch. As always, he is extremely helpful. We discuss Princess Margaret and I tell him about Elizabeth Longford saying that 'She has always been very good to *me*.' Hugo, Cecil Beaton's biographer, owns all his diaries and offers to let me have whatever extracts I may want about the Princess. He also gives me a great box of cuttings and a photograph of her attending a fashion show in 1951, in the days when the world was at her feet. In it, she looks like a fashion model herself.

Hugo entertained the Princess to lunch recently. He shows me the scrawled 'Margaret' in his visitors' book. How had she behaved at lunch, I ask. 'She has always,' says Hugo, 'been very good to *me*.'

24 May 1996

I have been asked, by a magazine, to write an article to commemorate the ninety-fifth birthday of Princess Alice, Duchess of Gloucester. So I write to the Princess to ask if she will give me an interview. I very much doubt that she will: her memory is going and I think that her recent move from Barnwell Manor to Kensington Palace has upset her. Her son, the Duke of Gloucester, has been criticized for making her leave her beloved Barnwell but I can see that the expense of keeping up the place must have been prohibitive. I get a reply today, from a lady-in-waiting, to say that the Princess will let me have her answer in a few days' time.

What I always find interesting in these talks with very old people are the direct links they give one with a remote past. For instance, Princess Alice, Duchess of Gloucester, once told me that, as a young child, she remembered seeing – in one of her grandfather's many great houses – a nursery maid washing the powder out of a footman's hair: the liveried footmen still powdered their hair before waiting at dinner.

And Princess Margaret told me that the ninety-year-old Princess Alice, Countess of Athlone, had once told her that, as a young girl, she had met an old lady who had attended the Duchess of Richmond's ball in Brussels on the eve of the Battle of Waterloo in 1815. Princess Margaret, whose sense of history is highly developed, delighted in that snippet of information. 'I used to tell my children to remember in *their* old age,' she said to me, 'that when they were young they had known someone who had known someone who had danced at a ball just before Waterloo.' (It is this same sense of the importance of the past that makes Princess Margaret bemoan the fact that the Queen Mother has never kept a diary. 'We've begged her to write down her memories, or even tape them,' she once explained to me, 'but she won't.')

In South Africa I once met a 93-year-old nun who had seen the Prince Imperial, son of the Emperor Napoleon III, at Mass in Pietermaritzburg, just before he set out to join the British forces fighting in the Zulu War of 1879. He was killed a few weeks later. So I must be one of the few people alive to have discussed the Prince Imperial with someone who actually saw him.

28 May 1996

A lady-in-waiting rings from Kensington Palace to say that an interview with Princess Alice will not be possible. HRH 'deeply regrets' turning me down as she thinks I am 'great fun'. However, it is arranged that I will go up to the Palace to speak to two of the Princess's ladies-in-waiting who will answer my questions. I rather gather that, once I am there, I will be taken in to greet the Princess and exchange a few words. A date is set for 7 June.

4 June 1996

A call from Kensington Palace cancelling my appointment on Friday. Apparently the Duke of Gloucester has objected to my proposed meeting with his mother's ladies-in-waiting. Brian and I suspect that he is afraid that they, or the Princess herself if I see her, will bemoan her move from Barnwell Manor.

28 August 1996

Up to London to attend to various odds and ends at the publishers. They all seem delighted with *Princess Margaret*. Michael O'Mara himself, whose relaxed manner masks a dynamic personality, has been very generous about the number of photographs, and the jacket – featuring a black and white picture of the Princess by Beaton – is superb.

As my train will not get me to Westbury until well after nine this evening, I decide to have a bite to eat at Paddington station. I choose lasagna and a half-bottle of white wine and settle myself at one of the tables outside the restaurant. Sitting there under the soaring glass roof of the station, I experience one of those rare moments of complete contentment. My private life is, as always, very happy and, if one is even a relatively successful writer, there are worse ways of earning a living.

It's probably the wine that brings all this on.

9 December 1996

A reporter on the *Evening Standard* telephones about my Princess Margaret book. Delighted by his interest and the publicity it will generate, I blithely answer all his questions. I suggest that he contact the publishers, who will undoubtedly let him have a copy of the book. He dutifully takes down the publishers' name and number.

I ring Lizzie – the publishers' publicity girl – to tell her the good news about the *Standard*'s interest. She is furious. Before calling me, the *Standard* had already called her about the book and she had refused to give the paper any information. This is because of the bidding for serialization which is currently in progress. Three newspapers – the *Telegraph*, the *Mail* and the *Express* – are hoping to serialize the book, and negotiations are at a delicate stage. So any revelations in the *Evening Standard* will seriously jeopardize the deal. All this is news to me. What exactly, she wants to know, have I told the *Standard*? I simply can't remember. Let's hope, she says grimly, that we don't lose the serialization, as a considerable sum of money is at stake.

In the end, the piece in this evening's *Standard* turns out to be pretty bland and the serialization is saved.

22 January 1997

I am usually very well but during the last few months I have had various things wrong with me. So my doctor arranges for a blood test.

I am in considerable pain when the photographer from *The Times* arrives today to take a picture to accompany the piece about me which is to appear in next Thursday's *Times*. The pain is hardly helped by the fact that he makes me pose in all sorts of awkward positions: perched on the arms of chairs, squatting beside the bookcase, even sitting on the floor. He takes no less than 144 shots, all of which leaves me feeling exhausted. God knows what I will look like.

26 January 1997

Go up to London to be given lunch by the woman journalist who is doing the profile on me for *The Times*. I limp all the way from Piccadilly Underground to the restaurant in Frith Street. The food is delicious, the wine dulls my pain a little but the interview doesn't go especially well. I feel that I am not able to give the interviewer the sort of thing she wants. I sense that she cannot find the right angle – or indeed, any angle – for the piece. Rightly or wrongly, I suspect that she is pumping me for information about other members of the royal family: that she isn't really very interested in the book itself. But I could be wrong about all this.

Glad to get home.

17 April 1997

This is my first entry for almost three months. On the evening after the day on which I arrived back from *The Times* interview in London, our doctor telephoned me. He had had the results of the blood tests. I have prostate cancer; there is no cure for this. A few days later I went to see a specialist. He told me that I had two years left to live. He suggested that I go travelling, say goodbye to my friends and settle up my affairs. He prescribed a course of tablets and a series of implants. This was followed by a biopsy and a bone scan. They both confirmed what he had said: that I have two years left. Other, of course, than Brian, I told no one about all this.

A week after I was told the news, I was plunged into the publicity for *Princess Margaret*, which was published on 7 February. For the following fortnight I was kept at it: going up to London, often for the night, to be on television and radio shows. On four occasions I had to go to the BBC in Bristol where, for literally hours on end, I was linked up to radio stations throughout the country. Through all this I was plunged in the deepest gloom. Perhaps my lowest point was on being woken by a 4.30 a.m. alarm call in a London hotel room in order to be at the ITV studios at 5.30. On arriving there, the place was locked and there Brian and I stood, in the biting February wind, waiting for someone to arrive. (On that particular programme I appear as bright as a button, as though I didn't have a care in the world. My friend Edna Moross dropped me a card to congratulate me for being 'on excellent form'.) Not even the fact that *Princess Margaret* quickly went on to the bestseller lists could lift my spirits. But, looking back, this forced activity was probably the best thing for me at the time.

Eventually, on Brian's insistence, I told our friends Andrew Wall and Werner Seehof about it. Werner immediately took me to meet a friend who had had prostate cancer for a couple of years and looked perfectly well. Andrew drove me to the hospital in Bath for my various examinations. I told my niece Sue Manby the news, and my nephew, Nick Manby, passed it on to my sister Peggy. I spent Easter with them, at Peggy's house near Canterbury, and came away feeling less desolate. Brian and I then spent a week at the Bristol Cancer Centre, at which my attitude towards my condition was transformed. I came away with a mass of complementary (as opposed to alternative) therapies and remedies.

From there we drove directly to Ticehurst in Sussex where we attended the '*Royalty Digest* Weekend' – an annual gathering of a hundred or so people interested in various aspects of royal history. It is organized by Paul Minet, publisher of *Royalty Digest* and of several reprints of my books. I had attended only one of these gatherings before and was astonished, and very gratified, by the high regard in which I am held by the people attending. Although appreciating that I was a biggish fish in a very small sea, I came away feeling considerably cheered.

Today, having had my course of tablets and two monthly implants, the doctor tells me that the results of the latest tests are very good. I am obviously responding extremely well to the treatment. At the moment, I feel fine. But, having been told to avoid as much stress as possible, I have decided to give up writing for a time and have returned the O'Mara advance on my next book.

London, 30 June 1997

To Hatchard's 200th Anniversary party, a black-tie affair attended by Princess Margaret. I am amused to see that all the copies of my book have been spirited away; presumably the sight of it – with its less than hagiographical tone – will offend HRH. Decide that I had better lie low as well.

She arrives very late, with her hair done up in an unbecoming sort of bun. But she looks very elegant, in a long, wide-skirted satin coat. She sports one of those huge royal handbags, this one shiny white with a tulip printed on it. While the rest of us drink sparkling white wine, she is given what looks like whisky, although the fact that her glass is carefully wrapped in a paper napkin makes it difficult to be certain. She chats away vivaciously to various people. How boring all this scrappy conversation with complete strangers must be for her. I talk to Elizabeth Longford, Hugo Vickers and Robin Piguet.

I slip away to meet Brian and as, post Bristol Cancer Centre, we are now vegans, we have a meal at Cranks – me in my black-tie outfit.

Frome, 14 July 1997

I do several telephone interviews for various Australian radio stations for *Princess Margaret*. A very cheerful chap this morning (it's always early in the morning) who confines his questions, almost exclusively, to HRH's drinking and smoking. 'You sound like a bit of a toff to me,' he says at one stage. I assure him that I am South African born, 'a fellow colonial' like himself. He loves this. 'Good on you, mate,' he exclaims.

7 September 1997

John Pescod, the vicar at St John's in Frome, telephones
to ask if I will give an address at the service to commemorate the death of the Princess of Wales. There has been
a great deal of public pressure, apparently, for such a
service. I agree, and although I was hardly a great admirer
of Diana, I write out something that should strike the right
note.

The church is packed mainly, I suspect, with people who
have never set foot in it before. Arrangements have even been
made to broadcast the service to an expected crowd outside.
I acquit myself pretty well, I think.

Such rivers of ink have gushed forth about Diana's life
and death that I don't feel that there is anything I can add.
A great deal of nonsense is being written, by people who
should know better, about how her death has marked a
turning point in the nation's history; how we are all going to
be more caring and sharing from now on. Diana undoubtedly
had what the Queen Mother had in her heyday – a strong
personal magnetism. It's a pity that the monarchy couldn't
have made better use of it. I think all of them, including
Diana, have been at fault.

22 October 1997

I get the results of my latest blood test. They are excellent;
in fact, the specialist calls them 'remarkable'. I ring my sister
Peggy to tell her the good news. She had been in two minds

about treating herself to a glass of whisky this evening; my news has decided her.

24 October 1997

Had a telephone call, a few days ago, from some television company in the States who are making a series called something like *Great Love Stories of the World* in which are to be included – among the likes of Antony and Cleopatra and Elizabeth Taylor and Richard Burton – Napoleon and Josephine and the Duke and Duchess of Windsor. It is about these last two couples that I have been contacted. So impressed, apparently, was the woman on the telephone by my 'intimate knowledge' that they have decided to send a team to Frome to record an interview.

They arrive today, with the usual mountain of equipment (am always worried sick about the wiring in this old house when they plug in innumerable appliances) and a set of questions. They are quite obviously not interested in nuances: these are being presented as deep and enduring loves, which is certainly not the case with either of my couples.

I am to be shot against a length of red velvet which is being dispatched, for some extraordinary reason and by special delivery, from New York. All morning there have been telephone calls from the States asking if 'the package' has arrived yet. It has not, nor by the time the team turns up, in the early afternoon, has it come. We wait and wait, telephone call follows telephone call and just as we decide to start without it, Brian comes pounding in with the package. It has been delivered, by a courier on a motorbike, all the way from Heathrow. What all this must have cost, I cannot imagine. And all for a length of the most ordinary – if by now creased – velvet which could have been bought in Frome for a couple of quid.

We are just about to start shooting when the telephone rings yet again. Assuming it to be the producer of the programme, I assure her that the velvet has arrived safely. There is a bemused silence on the other end of the line. The caller then explains that she is the woman who is doing the publicity for the American publication of *Princess Margaret*. She is calling to give me the good news that she has managed to get me on to the *Joan Rivers Show*.

27 October 1997

What a day. We are due to fly to South Africa tomorrow afternoon, for a six-week stay. Wake this morning to discover that the central-heating radiator in my study is leaking. Already there is quite a pool of water. I ring the gas people who cannot get anyone here until tomorrow morning.

There follows a telephone call from the woman doing the *Princess Margaret* publicity in the States. She has managed to get me on to an ABC television show. Can I spend the night in London and do the show, from ABC's London studio, first thing tomorrow morning? I refuse. For weeks I have been begging the American publishers for a publication date and have told them, again weeks ago, that I would be leaving for South Africa tomorrow. None of my letters has been answered. I explain all this to the contrite publicity woman.

In the afternoon she rings again. Does my plane leave

from near Frome? I explain that I have to get to Heathrow, which is several hours away. She says that the publishers will pay for a car to take me to the studio and then on to the airport. Again I refuse. I explain about the leaking radiator which must be fixed tomorrow morning before we leave. I don't think she believes this.

A third call. Can I postpone my flight? The publishers will pay whatever penalties this may incur. By now, the whole thing is taking on a nightmarish quality. I am usually the most amenable of people and I greatly enjoy doing publicity but as none of this muddle is of my making, I remain firm. It's just too complicated. I give her the date of my return to Britain and she will try to 'reschedule' the ABC interview.

Cape Town, 19 November 1997

We are spending a week in a suite at the Mount Nelson Hotel. All paid for by the Mount Nelson 100 Club, whom I address at a luncheon today. My sister Jean and my niece Jess are staying nearby in a holiday apartment; as the apartment has no bath, only a shower, Jean hides her sponge bag in her handbag and uses our luxurious bathroom.

My audience, made up of one hundred wealthy but altruistic women, is gratifyingly enthusiastic. I am effusively thanked by a woman who claims that her favourite book, which she reads and rereads, is my *The Swarm of Bees* — except, of course, that the correct title is *The Golden Bees*. I sign masses of *Princess Margaret*. All in all, a highly successful occasion.

Port Alfred, 2 December 1997

Prince Charles, with Prince Harry, is visiting South Africa. He is being treated, by the press and public, as a grieving heartbroken widower. Every speech and almost every news item refers to his recent 'tragic loss'. Even ex-cabinet ministers, on radio talk shows, pontificate on Charles and Diana. There is also an assumption here that the British public is concerned with little other than Diana's death. In interviews I am constantly being asked about the attitude of 'the British public' towards her death — as though everyone in Britain feels the same way.

After one of my talks I am asked if the present 'unpopularity' of the royal family is due to the fact that the late Princess of Wales was 'English' and the rest of the royal family 'German'. Very strange.

Port Elizabeth, 4 December 1997

I go into a shoe shop in Port Elizabeth and am served by a man who recognizes me. He tells me that he and I attended the same school and that he began work in this very shoe shop as soon as he left. He has worked here for almost fifty years and is due to retire soon. He tells me all about his family, his home, his car and his holidays. He is to make his first trip 'overseas' next year. He seems the very picture of contentment. Perhaps that's the way to do it.

Kirkwood, 6 December 1997

We spend a couple of days in Kirkwood, where I was born. I haven't been here for several years. It looks slightly different; the streets are now planted with palms and hibiscus, as well as jacarandas, which gives the place a more sub-tropical look. We stop the car outside the house where I was born and grew up. It is altered almost beyond recognition. Its style used to be what could loosely be termed standard Edwardian colonial: whitewashed walls, a pillared verandah and a corrugated iron roof painted dark green. Now it has been clad in that scourge of South African domestic architecture — a shiny, honey-coloured 'face' brick. A garage, built beside the house, makes it look like any ordinary suburban home.

In my mind's eye I can still see my always elegantly dressed mother coming out on to the verandah to greet me whenever I came back home: from boarding school, from university, from my years in London, from wherever I happened to be living at the time. In one of the back bedrooms, as a little boy, I used to sit painting pictures of kings and queens.

I cannot bear to go in. We drive on.

London, 13 December 1997

A 6 a.m. call wakes me at the Cumberland Hotel. It is from New York, from the man handling — or at least in some way responsible for — the postponed *Princess Margaret* interview for ABC later this morning. Am completely thrown by his questions, most of which concern Diana, and anyway, it's too early for coherent thought.

The interview itself seems to me disastrous. The ABC London studio is a vast, barn-like space, freezing cold and deserted except for a solitary man seated at one of the dozens of desks. I am put into a chair opposite a blank television screen and am asked questions, by someone in New York, through earpieces. By some miracle, I will appear on American television screens. The questions themselves are quite different from the ones I was asked earlier and quite different, also, from the sort of questions I am usually asked about the book. They mainly concern the Princess's fleeting associations with people like Mick Jagger, Elton John and the Beatles.

But I suppose it isn't quite as bad as I imagine.

Frome, 16 December 1997

The telephone interview with Joan Rivers. I start by telling her that I think she always looks lovely (which is true) and from then on it all goes swimmingly. We get on very well, or as well as one can over 3,000 miles of telephone cable, and the interview is lively and good-natured. She is, of course, as outspoken as ever. 'What a bitch! What a tramp!' she says about the Princess. My defence of HRH sounds pretty lame. Anyway, let's hope it helps to move some books in the States. Although I would have thought that, by now, Princess Margaret is rather a forgotten figure.

25 February 1998

With Diana's sudden death having caught the obituarists
unprepared, they're obviously determined not to be wrong-
footed again. In January – and at exhausting length – I was
interviewed for Princess Margaret's obituary for ITV, and
last week I did my stint for BBC television.

Yesterday's news – of the Princess's minor stroke on
Mustique – has meant a major flurry of activity for me:
television appearances, radio interviews and press articles.
Both BBC and ITV, ringing late last night, wanted me to
appear on breakfast shows in London this morning. This is
clearly impossible but ITV arrange for me to do it from
their studio in Bristol. I am due to be picked up, at home, at
5.30 a.m. to appear, for the first of three interviews, at 6.30
a.m. in the Bristol studio, twenty-five miles away.

As this house is difficult to find, I suggest that I wait in
the corner of the main car park. From 5.30 a.m., in the pitch
dark and bitter cold, Brian and I wait for the car to arrive.
As it has not appeared by five to six, I telephone the studio.
They assure me that the driver left over an hour ago. He
finally turns up just after six and we hare off, at breakneck
speed. Had he had difficulty in finding the car park, I ask.
No, he says, he couldn't find Frome.

20 March 1998

Andrew Lownie rang a few days ago to say that the American
publishers of *Princess Margaret* want me to write a book about

Diana. I refused. What is there left to say? I can bring nothing new to the subject; I am not particularly interested in her; I know no one in her circle.

None of this, apparently, matters. Andrew calls back the following day to say that the publishers have brushed aside all my reservations. They still want me to write the book. And they want it completed in three months! We decide that the only thing to do is to ask for so huge an advance that they will be forced to give up the idea. Andrew suggests one hundred thousand pounds, not dollars.

But by this morning, after a disturbed night, I have decided that we mustn't even employ this tactic. What if they agree to pay the advance? I will then be faced with the prospect of writing a book that I don't want to write, on a subject that I know very little about, about a person with whom I have very little sympathy – and all in three months. Impossible. I ring Andrew and we call the whole thing off.

But wouldn't £100,000 have been lovely?

London, 22 July 1998

Ever since the publication of *Prince Eddy and the Homosexual Underworld* in 1994, I have been getting fan letters from a quite different sort of correspondent. The most interesting letter was very much a voice from the past: it came from Dougie Squires, whom I had known over forty years ago. 'There can't be two people', he wrote, 'called Theo Aronson.' Dougie is now a highly successfuly choreographer but when we were last in touch, in 1951, things were very different.

I was then twenty-one, spending a year in Britain. Ted

Darroll and I had been hitch-hiking around the Continent for a few months and had arrived back in London almost penniless. So I underwent a couple of days' training to become a counter hand at J. Lyons and Company, who had restaurants and teashops all over the country in those days. At the training school I met Dougie Squires, then nineteen and just arrived from Nottingham. He intended to use his wages to further his ambition to become a dancer; I merely wanted to earn enough to keep myself afloat until I sailed back to South Africa at the end of the year. (I did indeed sail then, but the call of London was too strong, and I was back in Britain within two years.) Together, Dougie and I learned the skills – if that's what they were – to pour tea out of urns, to load trays and to scoop gravy on to the sausages and mash.

Dougie went on to greater things: among his many achievements was his own television series.

Today, forty-seven years later, we lunch at the Ivy: four of us – Dougie, his friend Antony Johns, Brian and I. Dougie and I assure each other that we look no different. It's all a far cry from eating beans on toast in the Lyons staff canteen.

Frome, 27 July 1998

A reporter rings to ask for my views on the 'modernization of the Queen's image'. I give him an off-the-cuff opinion, which seems to satisfy him.

What *do* I think? Well, for someone in her seventies to set out to change the public's perception of her is all but impossible. To try to repackage the Queen as some sort of informal, outgoing, caring-and-sharing Diana is ridiculous. The attempts to present her as an ordinary person in touch with her subjects' everyday lives have been frankly ludicrous. She steps out of her Daimler and goes into an all but deserted pub where she self-consciously takes a single sip of best bitter. Or she sits in someone's front parlour in hat and gloves, drinking tea and putting questions to some poor woman, rigid with nerves. It's all so toe-curlingly patronizing.

The Queen should play to her strengths. She is a reserved, dignified, conscientious woman, with a strong sense of dedication. She should be pictured doing what she does best: her duty. She should be shown at work, earning her living. She should be filmed at her desk, discussing things with her private secretary and going through her 'boxes'. She should be shown at an investiture, pinning on medals. She should be seen receiving ambassadors. The Queen is not a natural performer, but if she is filmed discreetly, going about the everyday business of monarchy, the public may appreciate that her role has some relevance; that she is a functioning head of state and not merely some relic from another age. The Queen's natural reserve should be turned into an asset: it should be used to show her as a serious-minded, hardworking, dedicated representative of an institution that still has a national role.

Anyway, for what it's worth, that's my opinion. I wish I'd thought of all this when the reporter telephoned.

St Petersburg, 9 August 1998

Brian and I are enjoying a two-week long cruise of the Baltic. Today we arrive in St Petersburg. The restoration of the spectacular architecture of this city continues but, on the debit side, the streets and squares are full of beggars and one of our guides regrets the passing of the days of free education and medical care. The change of name back to St Petersburg from the Leningrad of our last visit has been followed by the return of the remains of Tsar Nicholas II from Ekaterinburg. We go to the Cathedral of St Peter and St Paul where, in St Catherine's Chapel, lie the coffins of the Tsar, his family and his entourage which were placed here only last month. A striking example of the whirligig of time.

Stockholm, 12 August 1998

At Drottingholm Palace today we are in a salon whose walls are covered with portraits of the various sovereigns of Europe who were reigning during the 1860s. Among them is one of the Emperor Napoleon III, unmistakable with his hooked nose, cat's whisker moustachios and imperial beard. 'It doesn't *look* like Napoleon,' says one woman to another. 'That's because it's him in old age,' explains her friend confidently.

London, 29 September 1998

I come up from Sloane Square Underground station today and do something I haven't done for over forty years: I walk down Sloane Gardens to see the house, number 45, where I lived for two years in the mid-1950s. Sloane Gardens remains a canyon of red-brick houses but much smarter these days: window boxes, double-lined curtains, gleaming paintwork. It's clearly no longer the bedsit land of my day.

As one can't see my windows from the street, I go round the corner into Holbein Place and look up at the two little windows of my attic room. It was in this room that my career as a writer was born. I can pinpoint the very weekend. It was in mid-February 1956, and I was twenty-six years old. At the time, I felt that my life lacked direction. By then I had been a designer – commercial artist – with J. Walter Thompson (in Johannesburg and London) for just over four years. Although I was conscientious, a hard worker and had a certain talent, I lacked the necessary creative spark and certainly the enthusiasm to become a really successful designer. I felt that I should be dedicating my life to something else; to something that really interested and inspired me.

That weekend I finished reading a book which I happened to find in the local library. It was *Louis Napoleon and the Second Empire* by J. M. Thompson. Until then, I knew very little about the French Second Empire, other than what I had learned at school. But I found the book very interesting. In the last chapter, Thompson mentioned the 'flamboyant mausoleum', in Farnborough, Hampshire, which the exiled ex-Empress Eugenie had had built to house the remains of her husband, Napoleon III, their son, the Prince Imperial and, in time, her own.

So, the following Sunday, I took the train to Farnborough

and trudged up through the snow to St Michael's Abbey. It was visited by very few people in those days and, after a long wait, a very old monk, his bare feet in sandals, conducted me over the church. The sight of those three huge sarcophagi in the shabby, dimly lit crypt of the church fired my imagination. It is not too much to claim that it served as a turning point in my life.

From then on I read everything I could lay my hands on about the Second Empire and then about the whole Napoleonic saga. And it was during the following months that I became obsessed by the idea of making that pilgrimage to the burial places of the various Napoleons. Already doing my night job as a waiter at Au Père de Nico, I saved whatever money I could and, in September that year, I left that attic room for ever and set off, not only on my journey but towards a new career.

The dawn of my career as a writer was not, of course, the only thing that happened in that room during my two-year stay there. It's just as well that walls can't talk.

Frome, 22 October 1998

To the specialist today for my check-up. He is delighted with my progress. And so am I. I don't really know how long this happy state of affairs will last but we can forget his original prognosis of my having only two years to live.

'Go home', he says, 'and celebrate.'

EPILOGUE

OVER FIFTY YEARS have passed since, as a schoolboy, I first saw King George VI and his family on that sun-baked railway siding in South Africa. The British monarchy was then enjoying a period of considerable popularity. King George VI and Queen Elizabeth had emerged from the Second World War with their reputations greatly enhanced. In his tentative but valiant way, the King was trying to establish himself as, what he called, a 'People's King'. His Queen, in her inimitable fashion, was imbuing the monarchy with an entirely new warmth and elan. While retaining a certain royal mystique, the couple were making the Crown more accessible, more human. By luck, as much as anything, they had got the balance right.

In the half century since then, in spite of Queen Elizabeth II's dogged devotion to duty, this balance seems to have been lost. During my encounters with members of the royal family, I have been conscious of a certain – if unspoken – unease about the present state of the monarchy.

Understandably, women like the late Princess Alice, Countess of Athlone, and Princess Alice, Duchess of Gloucester, regretted the passing of the old certainties. Although both were unpretentious and adaptable women, their lives were firmly rooted in the grander days of the monarchy. Princess Margaret, on the other hand, epitomizes the modern royal dichotomy: the pull between being a princess and living her own life; between meeting the exacting standards of the monarchy and flouting its long-established conventions.

Prince Charles, more than any of them, seems to be torn between the privileges and unrealities of his inheritance and his often floundering attempts to adapt the monarchy to the very different world of the twenty-first century. It is when the media stops showing an interest in the doings of the royal family, he once said to me, that they would have to start worrying. Well, he need have no worries on that score. His every move is noted and analysed. One can only hope that his aim of becoming a 'People's King' in the mould of his grandfather, George VI, will still be achievable in the century ahead.

Only the Queen Mother, in her insouciant way, remains at ease in her position, enjoying both her luxurious way of life and her undiminished popularity. The new, pared-down monarchy of the future is one in which she will play no part. The institution which she served with such distinction may be changing too fast for her but she has no need of excuses. She can celebrate her centenary confident in the knowledge that she remains greatly admired.

'We just tried to do our best,' she once said to me. In its time, and for its time, that best was very good indeed.

Index